SARA ROWELL

Yvonne
Child of the Somme

AUSTIN MACAULEY PUBLISHERS™
LONDON • CAMBRIDGE • NEW YORK • SHARJAH

Copyright © Sara Rowell 2022

The right of Sara Rowell to be identified as author of this work has been asserted in accordance with sections 77 and 78 of the Copyright, Designs and Patents Act 1988.

All rights reserved. No part of this publication may be reproduced, stored in a retrieval system, or transmitted in any form or by any means, electronic, mechanical, photocopying, recording, or otherwise, without the prior permission of the publishers.

Any person who commits any unauthorised act in relation to this publication may be liable to criminal prosecution and civil claims for damages.

Cover design by Jan Bagley – Melbourne, Australia 2022.

Every effort has been made to trace all copyright holders of material included in this book. The publisher apologises for any errors or omissions and would be grateful to be notified of any corrections that should be incorporated in future reprints or editions of this book.

A CIP catalogue record for this title is available from the British Library.

ISBN 9781398481695 (Paperback)
ISBN 9781398481701 (ePub e-book)

www.austinmacauley.com

First Published 2022
Austin Macauley Publishers Ltd
1 Canada Square
Canary Wharf
London
E14 5AA

For Jan

ACKNOWLEDGEMENTS

I am indebted to the following organisations in particular for providing access to invaluable resources. With sincere thanks to the individuals named for all their help and support for this project.

Archives et Bibliotheque patrimoniale d'Abbeville
Hôtel d'Emonville
26, Place Clemenceau
80100 Abbeville
abbeville.fr/loisirs/archives-municipales
Eric Berriahi and Raphaële Jaminon Benoit.

Archives de l'AP-HP
Hôpital Bicêtre, Bâtiment Mathieu-Jaboulay
Secteur oranges – Porte 36
78 rue du Général Leclerc
94270 Le Kremlin-Bicêtre
archives.aphp.fr

Archives de Paris
18 boulevard Sérurier
75019 Paris
archives.paris.fr

Archives départementales de la Somme
61 rue Saint-Fuscien
80000 Amiens
archives.somme.fr
Jean-Michel Schill kindly took the time to check the records and discovered that Yvonne was an enfant de l'Assistance.

Imperial War Museum London
Lambeth Road
London SE1 6H
iwm.org.uk
I Was There oral histories – William Gillman – served with 2/4th and 2/2nd Bns London Regt (Royal Fusiliers) on Western Front 1918
Archive records of F.N. Pickett et Fils

Les Filles de la Charité de Saint Vincent de Paul
140 rue du Bac
75340 Paris
filles-de-la-charite.org
Sister Annie in Paris kindly supplied information about the hospices in Amiens and Abbeville.

Historial de la Grande Guerre – Péronne
Château de Péronne
Place André Audinot
80200 Péronne
historial.fr
Kindly gave permission to use a photo in their collection.

Historial de la Grande Guerre – Thiepval
8 rue l'Ancre
80300 Thiepval
historial.fr
Vincent Laude kindly provided a summary history of Thiepval before and after the First World War and shared photos and exhibition contents.

Metropolitan Police Archives
Shared Support Services – Heritage Centre
The Annexe, Empress State Building, Lille Road,
London SW6 1TR
PJ Aston provided information about Albert's police service record.

La Société des Antiquaires de Picardie
Kindly gave permission to use three photos in their collection.

Frédéric Turner
Author of 'Les Oubliés de 39-45, Les Britanniques Internés à Tost, Kreuzberg, Giromagny et Westertimke'.
Assisted with information about ex-servicemen who married French women they had met during the First World War, and also the round-up of British nationals in Nazi-occupied France in 1940.

Université de Picardie, Jules Verne,
Chemin du Thil
CS 52501
80025 Amiens
u-picardie.fr
Bertrand Depeyrot kindly took the time to tell me something about the university library building, formerly Hospice Saint-Charles, when I turned up unannounced in March 2018.

SPECIAL THANKS

This book would not have been possible without the wonderful support and encouragement of two of Yvonne and Albert's grandchildren Jan Bagley (Archie's daughter), whose curiosity inspired this project, and Chris Bagley (Gordon's son). Jan and Chris provided family background information, anecdotal stories and photos. Chris shared his own research into Albert Bagley's family history and introduced me to his uncle, Ron Bagley and his wife June who I had the pleasure of meeting in July 2019. Ron kindly shared his own recollections of his mother Yvonne. Thanks also to Jeanie Tummon (Chris's wife) who assisted with the Metropolitan Police Archives research. I am especially grateful to Jan for designing the book cover and the maps of Paris, Allery and the Somme region.

In Allery, Somme I would like to thank the staff of the mairie, and especially Catherine Fénelon, former elected representative, who took great interest in my project and helped provide valuable details. I am particularly grateful to Catherine for engaging Maryline Desjardins (granddaughter of Alfred Desjardins) with this story and introducing me to Frédéric Defente (grandson of Louis Allot).

Thanks to my husband Steve Rowell for his unfailing support during the research and writing of this book, and to my son Tom Rowell for his valuable feedback and help with translation when needed.

I would also like to thank authors Dave Derby and Hansa Pankhania for their feedback on an early draft of the manuscript.

Thanks also to David Barker for his valuable advice regarding publication.

Finally, thank you to my fellow members of Solihull Writers for their encouragement and feedback on extracts of the work in development. Special thanks to Jill Griffin, for reviewing the entire manuscript.

Thanks are due to everyone who helped me in any way to complete this book. Naturally, any errors remaining in the text are wholly my responsibility.

CONTENTS

Preface by Sara Rowell 9

A Book in Progress: 11

Part One: Paris, 1900 – 1901 15
   1: La Belle Époque 16
   2: 'Une Sixième' 21
   3. On the Brink 34
   4: Liberté, Égalité, Fraternité 40

Part Two: Infancy in Thiepval, June 1901 – January 1905 ...47
   5: The Childminder 48
   6: Innocence 58
   7: A Mother's Desperation 61

Part Three: The Allery Years, February 1905 – June 1916 ...71
   8: A Place to Call Home 73
   9: Growing Awareness 80
   10: War 91
   11: Childhood Ending 98

Part Four: Leaving Home, June 1916 – June 1922 103
   12: A Painful Parting 104
   13: The Shattering of Tranquillity 117
   14: Harsh Realities 123
   15: Fear and Peace 130
   16: Mistakes 135
   17: 'A Good Girl at Heart' 147

Part Five: Independence and Marriage, June 1922 onwards ...157
   18: Freedom and Trepidation 158
   19: Daring to Dream 162
   20. Encounter 164
   21: A Quiet Wedding 171

Part Six: Family Life, 1923 onwards 181
   22: Domesticity 182
   23: Leaving France 188

Epilogue: Searching for Marie 202

A generation before Yvonne's birth 205

Selected Bibliography 207

Index 209

Preface by Sara Rowell

YVONNE MILLET WAS not a famous person and her story is not unique. Yvonne's experiences growing up were typical of countless girls and boys born into poverty in France in the 19th and early 20th centuries. Yet their stories are seldom told. Their tales are uncomfortably full of hardship, deprivation, loneliness and shame. Yvonne was one of the lucky ones who survived infancy and was destined for life as a servant, like her mother before her.

During the course of my research I was struck by how little information I could find about the lives of servants in those times. Visiting historic houses in Paris and elsewhere in France, the existence of servants appears to have been airbrushed from history. In Britain, we have a fascination with life 'below stairs' and the period dramas to match. I have yet to visit an historic house in France where the servants' quarters are open for public viewing and their stories told. However, I did discover some valuable resources, including the excellent account by Paul Chabot of his grandparents' struggles as domestic servants (*Jean et Yvonne, Domestiques en 1900*).

Some rays of kindness and compassion do filter through the sadness of the saga. Yvonne's greatest good fortune as a child was to land with kind and diligent foster parents in the village of Allery, in the Somme region, where she also made lifelong friendships. Similarly, she had positive experiences of the Catholic church during her childhood. No doubt the church was one thing which felt constant and solid to Yvonne amidst the turbulence of her formative years.

Yvonne's life was in many ways remarkable. It was interwoven with the most dramatic events of 20th century history: the two World Wars. Her legacy is the large family she created with her husband Albert Bagley. I met their granddaughter Jan Bagley on our first day of secondary school in 1972. We have been firm friends ever since, despite living on opposite sides of the world for more than 30 years.

I was always aware that Jan's father was French, which was confusing for me as an eleven-year-old as he sounded completely English when he spoke. Jan occasionally talked about her '*Grand-mère*', whom she rarely saw. This French connection all seemed very unusual and a little exotic to me at the time, compared to my own British ancestry. We could never have imagined that decades later I would come to research and explore *Grand-mère*'s early life story. I did not set out to write a book, yet this is what has developed.

I hope my telling of Yvonne's story helps draw to attention the experiences of the countless others like her. For many, there was no happy ending. Although Yvonne made a lasting marriage with Albert, contentment was elusive. Happiness was hampered by the mental scars of her childhood and exacerbated by further disruption and trauma in her adult life. Naturally, this affected those closest to her. Never having met Yvonne, I have only got to know something of her character through conversations with Jan and other members of the family. She was not always an easy person to be around. Yvonne never sought to share her experiences with her children and they never had the chance to understand why she was the way she was.

Ultimately, this book is a tribute to all the children of early 20th-century France whose lives were scarred by the poverty of their origins. Perhaps now they will be better understood.

A Book in Progress:

Letter to Jan Bagley, Yvonne's granddaughter, July 2018

DEAR JAN,

Today, I am reviewing *Grand-mère*'s story before I share it with you in its entirety for the first time. It is 11 July 2018 and I'm in Paris, the 17th arrondissement, in a popular café. The floor-length windows are folded open onto the square des Batignolles, where there is a small park, green and shady, surrounded by typical 19th-century Haussmannian buildings. It's a warm summer's day, the weather much as it was when I began looking for traces of young *Grand-mère* nearly one year ago, and perhaps also like it was 117 years ago when, a few miles from where I'm sitting, she was born.

Researching and writing about *Grand-mère*'s early life has been an extraordinary project, coming at a time in my life when I was wondering 'what next?' It has given me a focus and the chance to experience what it is like to undertake a biographical writing project. It has also led me and Steve[1] to explore the Somme area, a part of France previously unknown to us. We have discovered beautiful towns and villages and, on the search for clues, have looked more intently at places we've visited than we would have done as casual tourists. We've seen things we would not otherwise have seen and had conversations with people we would not otherwise have met. It's been immensely rewarding.

It all began with the brief conversation you and I had when we were together in Tuscany, in May last year. As we strolled around the Boboli Gardens in Florence, we found ourselves talking about family backgrounds. Our conversation continued a few days later over coffee in Piazza del Campo, Sienna. Something in particular was on your mind: a mystery about your French grandmother, your *Grand-mère*. You knew little about *Grand-mère*, particularly her early life, because it was a closed

---

[1] The author's husband.

subject in the family, your Dad always reluctant to talk about her, as if he was concealing a secret.

You were wondering if my son Tom might be able to help translate *Grand-mère*'s birth, marriage and death certificates and, living in Paris, maybe find out a little bit more. This sounded to me like something I, rather than Tom, could explore for you, as a way of improving my French. It sparked an investigation that began in August 2017 and has become one of the most engrossing projects I have ever undertaken. I have learnt an incredible amount, not only about *Grand-mère* but also about the social history of France in the 19th and early 20th centuries, about the injustices suffered by women of this era and their struggles for survival, about the First World War on the Western Front, and about both the department of the Somme and Paris, where *Grand-mère*'s story begins.

Answers to the mystery of *Grand-mère*'s early life are tucked away in a weighty volume of official records, one of hundreds conserved in the archives of the city of Amiens, the capital of the department of the Somme, northern France. The book is large, needing both hands to lift it and to carefully open the cover. It is official-looking, hard-bound with a plain dark cover, the spine now brittle with age. Inside lie hundreds of pages of pre-printed forms, now beginning to loosen on their binding threads, containing notes handwritten by social workers in pen and ink, and sometimes pencil. They offer up factual information – dates, places, names – together with subjective observations which give small but revealing insights into the lives and personalities of children in the care of the state, including *Grand-mère* – Yvonne. I was possibly the first person in nearly a hundred years to turn its pages when I visited the archives last autumn. The staff there were very helpful.

Yvonne's records also include a slim, buff-coloured folder containing an ad-hoc selection of official documents, which the archivists also brought out from the store for me to read. The amount of information these records unlock is astonishing and they are the main source of the story that follows. Names and addresses in Yvonne's file enabled me to find out more about the characters in her early life through census and other archive records. Wider reading has given me the social-historical context. Discovering what happened has been like doing a complex jigsaw with many pieces missing. The overall picture has emerged, but we can only imagine what some of the lost details might look like. I have tried to paint a picture that breathes life into the story and gets as close to the truth as possible. Perhaps when you read what follows, you (or one of your relatives) might remember something more, a snippet of a conversation long

A BOOK IN PROGRESS: 13

ago or a memento tucked away in a drawer, suddenly taking on significance.

It is impossible to write about *Grand-mère* without bringing your *Grand-père* – Albert – into the story, and, of course, his part in the First World War. Their meeting was something of a miracle and dramatically changed the course of Yvonne's life. It is not entirely clear when and where exactly they first met; however, using documentary evidence to trace their movements, it does seem possible that it was, as you remember your father suggesting, during the war. I have found no evidence that Albert was billeted in the same location as Yvonne at any time, although their paths could have crossed in a military hospital when he was wounded.

Although Yvonne and Albert came from very different backgrounds, one thing that united them was their extraordinary and difficult experiences as young people, Yvonne because of the circumstances of her birth and both of them because of the First World War. They were survivors. I have developed the story in some detail up to the point of their marriage in 1923, and in outline up to 1938 when they left France. There is definitely more to explore, particularly the mystery of what exactly took Albert back to France after the war, and their years in the Lille area. By the time you were born in 1960, *Grand-mère* was 59, not much older than we are now, *Grand-père* was 63, and they had been married for 37 years. You knew them during their golden years as two kindly grandparents, a role I imagine they greatly enjoyed. I hope when you read this story of their early life you may come to know these two remarkable and brave people a little better, and understand more about the French heritage *Grand-mère* bestowed to you.

Love Sara x

Jan Bagley and Sara Rowell

Part One: Paris, 1900 – 1901

1: La Belle Époque

THIS IS THE story of a young French girl born at the start of the last century. Her name was Yvonne Millet. Even though this is Yvonne's story, she could not have told it herself, at least not in its entirety. Some of it she didn't know or was too young to remember. The rest she tidied into a simplified version of the truth. She smoothed it with a touch of romance until she could speak of it without fear of judgement or feelings of shame. The traumas she had suffered were too painful to think about, let alone share. They lay behind an outwardly forceful personality, tucked away in a far corner of her mind where they could not be easily disturbed.

Throughout her life, hurt and anger from her past sometimes leaked out unbidden in emotional outbursts, baffling those close to her. Yvonne's early life was a mystery to her family who knew nothing of the deep scars she bore. Had they known, could it have changed anything? Perhaps not, but they might have understood. None of us can change the past and our past will never let us go.

The story begins in Paris in 1900 with Yvonne's mother, a young woman of very limited means. Her name was Marie Millet. In Marie's Paris, 'La Belle Époque' ('the beautiful era'), as it later became known, was in full swing. It was the period, before the Great War, which history remembers as a golden era of fun, frivolity, decadence and optimism. Paris was famous the world over as the 'city of light', bejewelled with glamour and romance.

Marie lived in the heart of Paris, a short distance from rue de Rivoli, one of the smartest streets in the city. It is where the huge Louvre art museum, a former royal palace, is located. Rue de Rivoli runs west, parallel to the River Seine, to meet the avenue des Champs-Élysées at place de la Concorde. In 1900, as today, expensive shops lined these streets, offering the very best of Parisian luxury goods. Only the most elegantly dressed people were seen entering such establishments.

On the rare occasions Marie was free to wander along rue de Rivoli, she could only window-shop, never buy. It was a distraction and entertainment of sorts. She could marvel through the glass at the lavish displays

1: LA BELLE ÉPOQUE

of intricate gold jewellery and finest porcelain from Sèvres and Limoges. Dress shop windows artfully showing the latest fashions were another source of wonder and dreams. The sumptuous gowns in colourful silks, with tiny, corseted waists and trimmed with exquisite ribbons, lace and beading, were in stark contrast to Marie's own attire. Her clothes were plain, dark, functional and worn.

On fine days it was pleasant to follow rue de Rivoli to reach the Tuileries garden, where all strata of Parisian society took the air, and cut through to the right bank of the River Seine. Meandering westwards, Marie could gaze up at the Eiffel Tower, the latticed wrought-iron structure reaching gracefully into the sky. The tallest structure in the world, its ultra-modern design had shocked and amazed the world when it first opened for the city's Exposition Universelle (World Fair) in 1889. Poor people like Marie were rarely found among the queues of tourists, who came from all corners of the globe, waiting for a ticket to climb it.

In the summer of 1900, passing time on her afternoon off, Marie walked through packed streets. Lost in thought about recent events in her life, she was only dimly aware of the excited atmosphere all around her. There were more tourists in the city than usual.

It was a big year for Paris. The city was hosting its fourth Exposition Universelle and its first Olympic Games. The theme for the 1900 Exposition was 'Paris, Capital of the Civilised World' and was its most impressive and ambitious event yet. It opened in April 1900 and was a huge success, enjoyed by fifty-one million visitors by the time it closed in November. No expense was spared to showcase Paris to the world. The event spanned two huge sites, one on the champ du Mars at the foot of the Eiffel Tower and the other straddling the River Seine opposite Les Invalides, where two huge stone pavilions were specially built for the event, the Grand Palais and the Petit Palais. They are still standing today, housing important art galleries. The sites were linked by routes along the banks of the river. Tickets to the fair cost 1 Franc, too expensive for a great many Parisians who, like Marie, were living a precarious existence.

More affordable for Marie was a ride on the brand new Parisian Metro system, which after years in the planning was now under construction. The inauguration of Line One in July 1900 was a highlight of the Exposition. It ran from Porte Maillot on the west side of Paris through the heart of the city, then eastwards to Porte de Vincennes. With the streets congested with horse-drawn traffic, the new metro made it much easier to cross the city. For just 15 centimes in second class, anyone could board a train to enjoy the novelty of racing through the dark tunnels beneath the busy streets and by December, 17 million passengers had done so. Getting around the city was becoming easier for all.

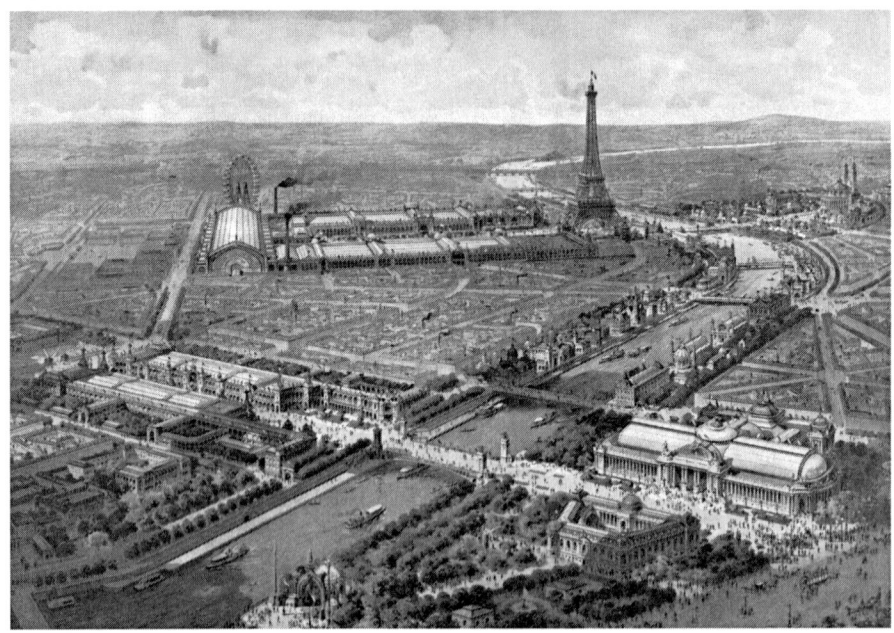

Panoramic view of the Exposition Universelle, Grand Palais and Petit Palais in the foreground on the right

To get away from the hustle and bustle of the city streets, Marie could venture further afield to Montmartre, high on a hill to the north. In 1900 it was still a ramshackle village dotted with windmills. Standing with her back to the construction site of a new church, the Sacré Coeur, she could enjoy one of the best views of Paris. The sprawling maze of city streets spread beneath her, glittering in the sunlight. Meandering around the cobbled streets, she could peer discreetly over the shoulders of artists at work on street corners and under the shade of trees. The images on some easels were unusual and daringly modern in their informal style. Among the artists in Montmartre in the autumn of 1900 was a nineteen-year-old Spaniard called Pablo Picasso, visiting Paris for the very first time. A community of artists had become established at Montmartre, drawn by cheap rent and the bohemian lifestyle, and the young Picasso wanted to join them.

Making her way home in the evening, Marie would pass groups of fashionably dressed Parisians heading to the Moulin Rouge cabaret music hall. The red windmill on its roof is still a landmark today, at the foot of Montmartre hill, on boulevard de Clichy. Opened in 1889, it was a magnet not only for rich Parisians but also for wealthy tourists, drawn by the risqué dancing. The gathering audience would not notice a woman like Marie as she passed by in the shadows. They were caught up in high spirits, eagerly anticipating the thrill of watching the cancan dancers, flashing their frilly undergarments with each high leg kick. Life had never been better for these people, the Parisian *bourgeoisie* (middle classes), who could afford to enjoy the city's pleasures. Their living standards were steadily improving at the dawn of the modern age and life was good. Life was not like this for Marie. It was not a Belle Époque for her at all.

Marie was one of the city's majority, one of the masses living in poverty. She could see the Belle Époque lifestyle up close and personal, but was separated from it by an invisible yet impenetrable wall, solid as thick glass. Marie was a *domestique* (servant), trapped by the dull drudgery that freed her bourgeois employers to enjoy comfortable, pleasurable, interesting lives. For her, as for most of the city's population of four million, life was a struggle, an existence more than a life.

Domestiques survived on low wages and lived miserably in cramped, unsanitary conditions. The wealthy male elite who occupied every position of power in society saw poor people not as individuals but as a homogeneous mass, a problem, a cause of ills. At the same time, they were slow to do anything about it, despite the efforts of reformers and influential people who spoke out, among them Victor Hugo, author of the 1862 novel *Les Misérables*. His tragic tale of Fantine and her daughter Cosette was based on the truth about the lives of working-class women and their children in 19th-century Paris. There were echoes of Fantine and Cosette in Marie's life.

Keeping people in poverty was a way to control the masses. George Orwell, in his book *Down and Out in Paris and London*, sums up the underlying attitude: '*For what do the majority of educated people know about poverty?... The educated man pictures a horde of submen, wanting only a day's liberty to loot his house, burn his books, and set him to work minding a machine or sweeping out a lavatory. "Anything," he thinks, "any injustice, sooner than let the mob loose". The mob is in fact loose now, and – in the shape of rich men – is using its power to set up enormous treadmills of boredom.*'

Gender inequality meant poor women struggled the most. They were paid considerably less than their male counterparts; however, they rarely questioned the unfairness of this. Most simply accepted it as how things were and it remained the norm until well into the late 20th century. Even today, of course, the struggle for equality goes on.

In 1900, around 200,000 people were working in domestic service in Paris, mainly women who had left their family homes in the countryside at a young age to escape rural poverty and find work. Marie Millet was one of them.

2: 'Une Sixième'

MARIE LEFT FEW traces of her existence behind, and there is only one clue as to her origins. The single piece of evidence pointing to where Marie came from is the record of her admission to a Parisian maternity ward in 1901. Amazingly, this has survived. Basic details of Marie's hospital stay were handwritten in a large, hard-bound register, today held by the Archives AP-HP[2] in Paris. It lists the hundreds of women who gave birth there in 1901 and Marie's record can be found roughly halfway through the volume. In the column headed '*Lieu de Naissance*', her place of birth is given as the commune of Annecy, in the department of the Haute-Savoie. This is an alpine region around 560 kilometres south-east of Paris. Listed on other pages are several more women from Haute-Savoie, a number of them *domestiques* like Marie.

These women had travelled considerably further from home than most in search of work; however, their regional accents were not uncommon on the streets of Paris. It may seem strange that anyone would travel all the way to Paris from the Alps when they could have found a job in Lyon or another large city closer to home. Yet Paris was a huge draw for young people from poor rural areas in search of higher wages and adventure. The growth of the railways in the 19th century made it increasingly easy to follow a dream.

For many girls, the dream was to work in the capital long enough to return home with money and more sophisticated ways. Some girls followed another member of their family, a brother perhaps, who helped find a position ahead of her arrival or at least let her stay with him until she found her feet. Other girls turned to regional associations and welcome centres, which were often led by charities and set up near railway stations, to help job seekers arriving in the capital from the provinces. Marie would have arrived in Paris at Gare de Lyon railway station, and there may have been an Haute-Savoyard welcome centre nearby, which she turned to for help. Arriving in the city alone with no pre-arranged plan was risky

---

2   The archives of Paris' public assistance and hospital services.

for a young woman from the country. The cost of train fares over such a distance was expensive, and she would have to earn the train fare home.

Despite the evidence in the hospital record, there is a question mark over whether Marie really was from Annecy. No clear trace of Marie Millet exists in the Haute-Savoie birth records, which are freely available online. In the 19th century, Millet was a rare name in that part of France, but more common in the north. Perhaps Marie had not travelled so far after all and that an error was made on the hospital register.

Record-keeping was unreliable in those days. The handwriting in the register is neat, in the same ink by a single hand, the details of the mother and baby entered at the same moment. This indicates the entries were transcribed from patient notes, after mother and child had left the maternity ward. Could it be the administrator got distracted when he wrote up the register, and put the wrong information for Marie under '*Lieu de Naissance*'? It is impossible to say.

The 1901 hospital register claims Marie was aged 28 when admitted to the maternity ward. But there is evidence elsewhere to suggest she was older, perhaps 30 in 1901. There is little doubt she worked as a *cuisinière* (cook), since this is recorded on at least three documents. She may have been in service in the city for a number of years, beginning as a maid and rising to the level of *cuisinière*.

Far right: 4 rue Berger, corner of rue Saint-Denis, c. 1905

2: 'UNE SIXIÈME'

There is firm evidence of where she lived and worked. Marie's job was a live-in position in a private home, an apartment at 4 rue Berger in the 1st arrondissement. This was (and still is) a prosperous district close to the historic heart of the city. No records exist to identify Marie's employers or how many people formed the household she served. Censuses in Paris prior to 1926 only counted numbers of people, recording nothing about identities. By the time of the first detailed census in 1926, 4 rue Berger had become a lodging house, according to a business directory of the day, mainly for young men who had come to work in Paris from as far afield as Spain and Poland. But in 1901, the building was an apartment block, with a shop at street level, in the bustling market area of Les Halles. It is still there today, occupying a plot on the corner of rue Berger and rue Saint-Denis[3].

The large stone building spans six floors, not a fancy apartment block compared to many in Paris, the architecture quite plain. In Marie's time, the ground floor shop was a greengrocer's, listed in the Didot-Bottin business directory of 1901 under the name of Gaudin. By 1905, the greengrocer's had changed hands and was now Lallemand & Carsaul; the sign bearing this name can be seen clearly in a photo of the building taken around this time. Above the shop, there were apartments on each of the five floors. The heads of households living in these apartments were perhaps up-and-coming merchants at Les Halles, not the wealthiest people but certainly *bourgeois*, or at least *petit bourgeois* (lower middle class).

Marie entered the building through a door opening directly from the street into a communal entrance hall with a tiled floor. From the hallway, Marie climbed a dimly lit wooden spiral staircase up through the building. The household she served lived on one of the higher floors. These apartments had the highest ceilings and the better-off residents, who could afford to employ *domestiques*. This is not, however, where Marie slept. At the end of her working day she would continue up the wooden staircase to the sixth floor, where all *domestiques* working in the building, male and female, lived together unsupervised.

Parisian *domestiques* were known as '*les sixièmes*' because they lived on the sixth floor, the very top of most Parisian apartment buildings. There was no lift. Today's *sixièmes* are young professionals, renting tiny apartments created in the attics that were once the servants' quarters.

Marie was a '*sixième*'. Her bed was directly under the roof and she

---

3 The address is now 45 rue Saint-Denis.

shared this attic space with the other *domestiques* at 4 rue Berger. When people took a lease on an apartment, it would come with a '*cave*' in the cellar, to provide extra household storage, and a cheerless cubbyhole in the attic for a *domestique* or two to sleep in.

Typically the bourgeoisie would not bother to inspect the servants' quarters before taking the lease, and the *domestiques* themselves would not dare to ask to see the accommodation before accepting the position. In any case, the servants' quarters in 19th-century Parisian apartment blocks were much the same all over the city. In some buildings, the *domestiques* removed the partition wall separating the living quarters from those in the block next door, creating a kind of continuous sixth-floor street under the rooftops.

Tens of thousands of apartment blocks were built this way and it wasn't until after the Great War that architects began to design accommodation for *domestiques* with any thought to their comfort. These 19th-century apartment blocks still exist right across Paris. The attic servants' quarters give the city its distinctive skyline, with dormer windows and skylights puncturing grey slate and zinc-clad roofs.

❖ ❖ ❖ ❖ ❖

When she climbed the stairs at night, Marie reached her room along a claustrophobic and poorly lit corridor off the sixth-floor landing. The room itself, one of a few, was created by partitioning the attic. Each room was roughly four metres square. There was just about room for Marie to move around her narrow iron bed, at the foot of which stood the small trunk with which she had travelled from home. In here she kept her few possessions, of little monetary value, yet to her very precious. There was a set of out-of-season clothes stored away until needed, together with a 'Sunday best' outfit, plus small keep-sakes.

Photos of family back home might be pinned to the thin wooden walls, together with illustrations cut from a magazine, in an effort to personalise this meagre space. A pitcher and bowl for Marie's simple daily toilette stood on a small washstand and she kept a chamber pot under her bed. At night she hung her shawl and skirt on a rough peg on the wall or threw them over an old wooden chair in the corner. Items of broken furniture or other junk belonging to the household typically filled any remaining space.

The roofline of 4 rue Berger suggests particularly poor, but not untypical, accommodation. Only one dormer window and one skylight can be

2: 'UNE SIXIÈME'

seen serving the whole attic space. There was hardly any ventilation or daylight inside and Marie's only light source after dark was a single candle in a battered tin holder. Poorly insulated, the attic was sweltering hot in high summer and desperately cold in the depths of winter, when at night it was tempting to lie together with another person simply for warmth. In the countryside, *domestiques* were known to take a dog from the yard into their attic room on a freezing night to help keep them warm.

Marie had little privacy or comfort, other than somewhere to lay down at the end of each exhausting day. For an hour or two before bed, she might have the companionship of the other *domestiques* in the building. They would arrive up in the attic at different times of the evening, depending on when they finished work. Hours were long, typically seven in the morning until ten at night, or later. Those who wanted to sleep were often disturbed by noisy talk or bawdy behaviour on the other side of the partition. A woman might discover her male neighbour had poked a hole through the flimsy wall separating them and was spying on her. All she could do was block the hole with scraps of paper and hope they stayed put.

Marie and her fellow *domestiques* had little time or energy to keep their living quarters clean and in any case had very restricted means. For some domestiques, bedding, and even clothing, went unwashed for months on end. If they were lucky, a single cold water tap served the entire floor; otherwise, they carried water up in buckets from the courtyard, six flights of stairs below.

Maintaining personal hygiene was difficult. Marie washed with a cloth rinsed in a bowl of cold water. In more modern blocks, there was one shared toilet on the servants' floor (of the squatting sort), otherwise *domestiques* used a chamber pot with nowhere convenient to empty it. Even in the mansions of the upper classes, plumbing for toilets and bathrooms was only just beginning to be installed in the early 1900s.

Anyone venturing into the servants' quarters during the day was greeted by a squalid scene and a fetid air. Beds were left unmade and chamber pots not emptied because the *domestiques* had risen early, dressed quickly and hurried downstairs to begin another long gruelling day. Living like this for months and years on end became increasingly hard to bear, both physically and psychologically.

The wealth of a household determined the number of *domestiques* they employed. The lower middle classes (*petite bourgeoisie*) could usually only afford one *domestique* while those higher up the social scale could employ more. Having *domestiques* was a status symbol, a sign of membership of the bourgeoisie. In an age where to live comfortably involved huge quantities of time-consuming manual labour, servants were the domestic appliances of the day, sparing those who could afford it from doing the work themselves.

The worst employers treated their *domestiques* as barely human, working them to the point of exhaustion, sending them to the attic overnight and expecting them back in service early the next morning. Some would even boast to their friends about how harshly they treated their *domestiques*. Others were kind, decent people and grew fond of their *domestiques*, who became almost like members of the family, even eating their meals with them at the same table.

How *domestiques* were treated, of course, depended on the temperament of their employers rather than their wealth; there were as many good and bad masters and mistresses in the provincial châteaux of the upper classes as in the Parisian apartments of the bourgeoisie. Even if Marie's employers were kindly disposed, treating her well during the day as she cooked for them in their comfortable apartment, she still returned at night to squalor up on the sixth floor. Had they bothered to take a look, they would have been shocked to discover what conditions were like up there. It was a case of 'out of sight, out of mind'. Most *domestiques* dared not complain.

As Marie was a *cuisinière*, this suggests there was at least one other *domestique* in her household to do the other chores, a male valet or a female *'femme de chambre'*. Despite the grand titles, these roles were similar and could encompass almost anything, from helping their master or mistress dress, mending clothes, cleaning and making the beds to fetching and carrying and opening the door to visitors.

In a typical bourgeois household, it was rare to find more than three servants and often there was only one, usually female. The vast majority of *domestiques* in 1901 were women. We can assume it was another girl from the countryside who worked alongside Marie. Women who were the sole *domestique* were known as a *'bonne à tout faire'* ('good for everything'), or *'bonne'* for short, and had a very tough job. They undertook all household duties, ranging from cooking and cleaning to laundry and even childminding. Although Marie was only responsible for getting the meals, her job was nonetheless demanding: tiring, monotonous, disheartening and at times very stressful. It was best for both women if they tried to get along well, helping each other finish the daily chores quickly and without incident.

The kitchen in which Marie toiled all day was cramped and poorly ventilated. Leaving the window open in all weathers was a necessity. The heat from the range and steam from simmering pans created a humid atmosphere, said to contribute to a number of ills, including the famous 'rhumatisme des cuisinières'. Marie may have been unaware of a more lethal risk: carbon monoxide poisoning from the gas lamps that lit the kitchen. Opening the window may well have saved her life.

Nineteenth-century apartment buildings were not designed with enough care regarding how they would function for their inhabitants, especially the servants. The rooms with the best views were for the master and mistress to enjoy. In most blocks, the kitchen where the servants toiled was at the back, typically overlooking an interior courtyard, which was open to the elements and let in some light to an otherwise dark space. *Domestiques* shook rugs and dusters out of the courtyard windows, sending dust wafting down and into open windows on the lower floors, where it settled on any food left out on kitchen counters. The courtyard was also usually where the water pump for the building was found, together with fuel stores and rubbish bins.

However, a street plan for rue Berger, in the Paris archives, shows number 4 did not have an inner courtyard. The corner plot naturally gave the building light and air on two sides without the need for one. The servants at number 4 went into the street to fetch water and take out the rubbish, and down into the basement to collect coal for the range and the fire.

Marie earned around 50 Francs a month for all her hard work (the equivalent of around £220 to £300 today).[4] Her wages, though better than more junior *domestiques*, were lower than the average for an unskilled female worker because, in domestic service, her accommodation and food were provided. The *femme de chambre* earned less than Marie, the status of a *cuisinière* being higher. Marie's working clothes and laundry were also included in her salary, or at least the provision of the clean aprons she was expected to wear every day. She undoubtedly earned more than in a similar role in the provinces. She could hope for an occasional pay rise in recognition of good work, and if she was lucky tips for extra duties, or even a small gift for her birthday. If her employers were decent people, and she was a good, honest worker, they would not want to lose her. *Domestiques* usually had a bit of spare cash to spend on a few modest comforts and treats. If Marie was careful and sensible, she also put money away in a

---

[4] Rough estimate. Information is hard to come by to establish accurate conversion rates.

savings account as a cushion against hard times, which were inevitable given the precariousness of her employment and living arrangements.

There was little chance for *domestiques* to have a personal life because of the long working hours, which made them more or less prisoners of the family they served. It was a lonely and demoralising existence for many, living far away from their families. Their poverty was of money and time, depriving them of so much that makes life worthwhile: freedom, friendships, a sense of well-being, the ability to discover who they were. Work consumed them and suppressed their individuality, their hopes, their dreams. The possibility of marriage was remote, the challenges of making even a very modest home under the same roof with another *domestique* almost insurmountable. Sharing a single bed in a cramped room on the *sixième* might be the most a married couple could aspire to and the arrival of a child posed a whole new set of difficulties. Resigned to never being able to marry, it was not uncommon for male *domestiques* to turn to prostitutes.

Some *domestiques* sought solace in the Christian faith. However, they could only attend church before the working day began. Special services were held for them at 6 o'clock in the morning. Unsurprisingly, these were not well attended. Others turned to drink. There were some bars in Paris in the 1900s where the customers were all *domestiques*, drinking for a few hours of release on their night off, or to dull the pain of their virtual enslavement. George Orwell in *Down and Out in Paris and London* describes how, for many low-paid Parisians, '*unmarried and with no future to think of, the weekly drinking bout was the one thing that made life worth living*'. The concept of human rights was still decades away. In 1948 the Universal Declaration of Human Rights recognised the terrible wrongs of Marie's kind of existence. It included the right to rest from work and relax.[5] Marie had little opportunity for either.

As a *cuisinière*, Marie was less socially isolated than other *domestiques*, whose role largely confined them to the place where they served. Early each morning, after serving a *petit déjeuner* (breakfast) of bread with a bowl of strong milky coffee or hot chocolate, she descended the stairs to the street. Gripping the rail with one hand, with the other she hitched her ankle-length skirts a little while keeping hold of a large wicker basket. This was empty apart from a shopping list for the meals she must prepare that day. Her long hair was scraped back off her face into a tight bun and

---

[5] Article 24.

she wore a woollen shawl around her shoulders, pulling it close against the chill as she stepped outdoors.

Marie was a familiar figure in the busy neighbourhood around Les Halles, the city's chief fresh food market. It was Paris's equivalent of London's Covent Garden and had traded on the same site along rue Berger for 800 years. An 1895 painting of Les Halles by Léon Lhermite, on permanent display in the Petit Palais, depicts the bustle outside the market building. It is easy to imagine Marie in the scene, with the crowd pressed close around her as she made her way from stall to stall. A series of 19th-century paintings by Edouard-Jean Dambourgez evoke the atmosphere inside the glass-roofed market building. One titled *The Cream and Cheese Merchants of Les Halles* shows a row of women, some *cuisinières* like Marie, queuing up with their baskets ready to make their purchases. She frequented the same shops and stalls every week, either because her mistress told her which ones to buy from, or more likely because she knew which traders offered the best incentives.

'The Cream and Cheese Merchants of Les Halles' by Edouard-Jean Dambourgez

Cuisinières were important customers and traders vied for Marie's loyalty. The relationship was mutually beneficial. Marie got more than a smile and enquiries after her health when she went shopping, welcome though that was. She also received as much as five per cent off the price of her purchases. She pocketed the saving for herself. Most traders offered regular customers money back for every Franc spent and this was known as *'le sou du franc'* (a sou was worth 5 centimes). Employers knew this practice went on and grumbled about it, but they were powerless to stop it. Provided the quality of the provisions Marie bought was acceptable to her master or mistress, there was little they could do to deny Marie this perk.

Her daily shopping list included cheese, cream, eggs, meat, fish, fruit and vegetables, depending on the choice of dishes for the day, which were agreed with her employer the evening before. The menu varied according to the seasons. Marie knew, for example, that *cuisses de grenouilles* (frogs' legs) were at their best in May and that Reblochon cheese, deliciously sweet from the wild flowers and herbs on which the cows grazed, would arrive from the Haute-Savoie in July.

❖ ❖ ❖ ❖ ❖

On days when her employer was entertaining, Marie's list was extra-long, her basket was heavier and her workload increased dramatically. She was forced to race against the clock. The Parisian bourgeoisie regularly invited friends into their home for a lavish meal to show off their wealth and good taste. Expectations were high and nothing less than perfection would do from Marie, who toiled all day to prepare multiple courses, knowing her employers' reputation for entertaining rested in her hands. After returning from the market, she darted about the kitchen juggling knives and skillets, sieves and rolling pins, pots and pans, with a frown of concentration etched across her sweating brow. *Cuisinières* dreaded the news that there would be guests coming for dinner, which greatly added to the stress of their day. And they knew it would be a very late night.

While Marie slaved away in the hot kitchen, the *femme de chambre* prepared the *salle à manger* (dining room), lighting the fire to warm the room if necessary. She set the table for the family and their guests, first spreading a crisp white cloth and placing a small vase of fresh flowers in the centre of the table. Marie briefly left the kitchen to check the cutlery was polished to perfection, the claret glasses spotless and each setting was properly aligned. As she moved briskly around the table she kept a close eye on the ornate mantlepiece clock, its elegant hands tick-ticking away the time she had left before dinner must be served.

When the guests arrived in the early evening, they were admitted by the *femme de chambre*, who showed them into the *séjour* (sitting room). This was the room into which Marie was summonsed each evening for instructions about the next day's meals. Like the rest of the apartment, it was furnished in the style fashionable with the bourgeoisie throughout the 19th century. The look was heavy, fussy, with dark, solid furniture and densely patterned carpets. An abundance of ornaments and knick-knacks sat on tapestry or velour covers protecting the mahogany or marble-topped furniture beneath. Lampshades trimmed with pendulous beading complemented chairs in plush fabrics edged with fringing. The tall French windows were draped with velvet and brocade curtains, tied back with thick tasselled cords. On one side of the apartment, the windows overlooked the ancient fountain, the *'fontaine des Innocents'*, on rue Berger while on the other side the view was of Haussmann buildings along rue Saint-Denis. The apartment was certainly not as grand as those to be found on rue de Rivoli or place Vendôme, a short distance west of rue Berger. Marie's employers aspired to the elegance of these homes. Yet the contrast of their comfort with the dingy attic rooms for the servants could hardly be greater.

Marie had to ensure the meal was ready to be served at the time agreed with the master or mistress. The *femme de chambre* then announced dinner was served and the guests made their way into the *salle à manger* to take their seats. It was the job of the *femme de chambre* to serve the food, and the hors d'oeuvres came first. Going back and forth to Marie in the kitchen, she relayed a feast to the table of soup, a selection of *bouilli* (boiled meat), fish, entrées, followed by the principal dishes of game or *rôti* (roast meat), vegetables and salad.

Later she served something sweet Marie had prepared, maybe *crème caramel* or *mousse chocolat*, and fruit according to the season. To round off the meal she served strong, black coffee and cognac in the *séjour*, over which the diners sat long into the evening. Marie and the *femme de chambre* ate as and when they could, hurriedly consuming leftovers from each dish before pressing on, longing for the last guest to leave and the working day to be over.

❖ ❖ ❖ ❖ ❖

Shopping daily was a necessity in the era before refrigeration and on ordinary days, when there was not quite so much pressure, Marie could chat with the people she met out and about, the traders and other customers waiting with her in the queue to be served. She got to know other *cuisinières* this way. Gradually, she also made friends and acquaintances among *domestiques* working in her own and neighbouring buildings, although they could rarely snatch more than a few minutes in one another's company. In times of trouble, '*les sixièmes*' supported one another as best they could. They shared information and advice, and if nothing else, could offer each other words of consolation and a shoulder to cry on. They did not have the freedom, time or resources available to do more for one another.

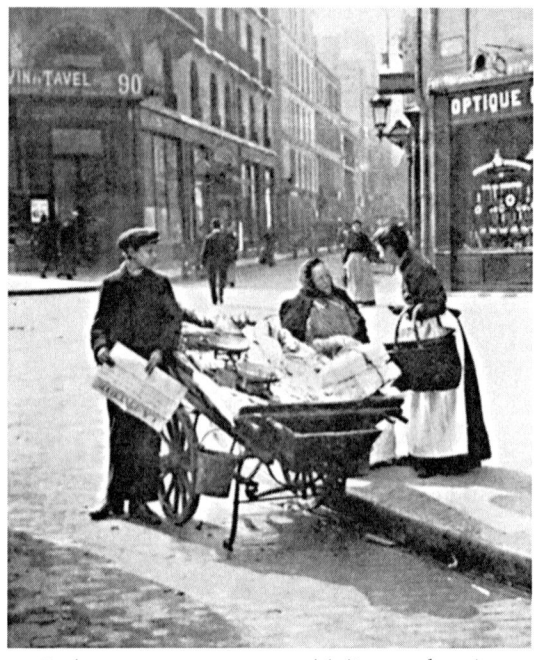

Paris street scene c.1900: a cuisinière out shopping

Despite Marie's shortage of leisure hours, romantic encounters were possible. It was easy for a woman in her circumstances to fall for a man showing interest in her, offering comfort and kindness in her otherwise hard, monotonous life. Marie was vulnerable to opportunistic men who would seduce women with promises they later broke. Certain men were particularly attracted by the sight of a servant girl in her white apron – it was a fetish. Some even deliberately rose early to go to the market in the hope of catching the eye of a pretty *domestique* as she shopped for groceries. This predilection surely gave rise to the saucy French maid caricature of popular culture, behind which were real women, often young inexperienced country girls, whose lives could be ruined by such men.

Under the roof she called home, Marie was just as vulnerable. Sixth-floor servants' quarters were renowned for promiscuity. Marie inevitably received advances from male servants sharing the attic at 4 rue Berger, welcome or otherwise. There was little privacy and it was difficult for a

2: 'UNE SIXIÈME'

young woman living in these conditions to protect herself. It's unlikely the door to her tiny bedroom had a functioning lock.

Marie's time off was precious, amounting to one or two Sunday afternoons and evenings a month at best. Harsh employers were reluctant to grant their *domestiques* any time off, or did so begrudgingly. Desperate to escape the confines of the attic, Marie ventured out into the city in her free time. It was a chance to seek out the company of other young people and find whatever social life she could. Mostly she mixed with other *domestiques*, drawn together by their lot in life. Sharing news, unburdening the injustices of their week, and comparing wages and working conditions took the edge off their loneliness. They met wherever free public entertainment could be found.

Circuses and fairs were frequently held in the city and were popular with all social classes at the time. For a couple of sous, Marie could ride on a carousel or goggle at highly dubious attractions like the fattest woman in the world, the girl with three legs or the bearded lady. Public dances in the city's parks and squares also drew huge crowds on summer afternoons. One of the most popular, and infamous, was at the Moulin de la Galette on rue Lepic in Montmartre. Its laid-back atmosphere appealed to an eclectic crowd, among them workers, students and bohemians from the neighbourhood.

Naturally, the artists of Montmartre were among the clientele, finding plenty at the *'bal'* (dance) to inspire their creativity. Pierre-Auguste Renoir's 1876 painting *Bal au Moulin de la Galette* is considered one of his most important works. Although painted 25 years or so before Marie's time, it is easy to imagine her in Renoir's lively, romantic scene of young people enjoying one another's company in the dappled sunlight. Couples hold each other close in their arms as they move in time to the music. One or two of the men appear to be stealing an illicit kiss.

There was also a more decadent side to these dances, which sometimes got out of control and attracted the attention of the police. Henri Toulouse-Lautrec, Maurice Utrillo and Kees van Dongen were among the artists who captured a seedier scene. Pablo Picasso also painted the *bal* at the Moulin de la Galette during his visit in 1900.

For *domestiques* like Marie, these dances were an oasis of colour and excitement in their otherwise dull and dreary lives. Naturally, romances blossomed as the band played into the night. But romance was a risky affair. For a poor woman in Paris in 1900, it could lead to devastating consequences.

3. On the Brink

SOMETIME DURING THE autumn of 1900, Marie became pregnant. This potentially spelt disaster for her.

Falling pregnant was the biggest worry of all for a *domestique* and this was not the first time it had happened to Marie. Her mind was in turmoil, knowing her job and her lodgings at 4 rue Berger were immediately at risk. She was a step away from destitution as an unemployed, homeless, single mother. *Domestiques* lived in fear of being sacked and put out on the streets for the slightest misdemeanour. Marie knew her employers could send her away once they knew of her condition.

Last time, they had shown compassion but she hardly dared hope they would do so again. For records show Marie had given birth to a daughter earlier the same year. Henriette Yvonne Marie Louise Millet was born on 29 March 1900 at 4 rue Berger. A midwife called Marcelle Lux, who lived nearby, attended Marie and registered the birth for her the next day. Mercifully, Marie had kept her job and place to live after Henriette's birth by arranging for a childminder to take her. Against the odds, she had held her life together. But tragedy was just around the corner. Henriette had died of convulsions in the childminder's care on 10 June 1900. She was just 10 weeks old.

It is impossible to know whether the same man fathered both Henriette and the new child on the way. Henriette's father was not named on her birth record. Marie carried on living and working at 4 rue Berger after Henriette's birth, so if the father also lived there, another servant perhaps, she had not felt the need to move away. Although employment was precarious for *domestiques*, Marie's skills were in demand. Once she had sorted out care arrangements for Henriette, she could have found another job if necessary. There were plenty of positions for good *cuisinières* in Paris, provided they did not have a baby in tow.

It was not unusual for the master or his sons to father a child with his servant girl, the result of constant pestering, persistence or rape. A *domestique* could expect no support from such men and had no course of redress. They were silenced by their need for work and shelter and

3. ON THE BRINK

the lack of alternatives. Some even found themselves dismissed, on the grounds of their pregnancy, by the very man who had made her pregnant. It was a convenient way of covering up his behaviour. If his wife had any suspicions at all, she would take matters into her own hands and dismiss the girl herself. Marie stayed where she was, so it is unlikely her master was Henriette's father.

The father of Marie's next child is another question. Again, there is no way of knowing who he was because Marie left no record of his identity. Perhaps he had promised her a future together, even marriage, then deserted her on learning she was pregnant. If he was also in domestic service, he may have walked away because of the sheer hopelessness of their situation. Perhaps he was already married. There are numerous possible scenarios, all commonplace for poor women in Paris at that time.

Marie's need for affection and intimacy is easy to understand and any man paying her attention would have been hard to resist, even when this risked unwanted consequences.

Whoever the father was, he knew the law protected him. Legally, unless he chose to acknowledge his child and be named on the birth record, he was absolved from any parental responsibility. The law also forbade Marie from seeking maintenance from him. These laws were designed to protect the inheritances of the wealthy, but had devastating consequences for poor mothers and their children. Not only were single mothers unable to seek support from the father, wage inequality meant they had fewer resources to parent alone. In Britain, by contrast, the law did allow mothers to pursue the father for maintenance through the courts. However, it wasn't until 1912 that the law began to change in France, allowing single mothers to pursue their child's father for financial support in some circumstances.

Marie's situation was far from unusual. At the turn of the century, around a third of all births in Paris every year were to single mothers. This statistic stemmed from widespread poverty, subjugation of women and no access to birth control except for the wealthy. Typically, of all women giving birth, around half were in domestic service. Marie undoubtedly knew other single women in the neighbourhood dealing with unplanned pregnancies. She was better informed than most about what to do, not only because she had been in this situation before. Going out daily to shop, she picked up all kinds of news, information and gossip. *Cuisinières* were central to the female servants' network because their work took them out and about in the neighbourhood. Other *domestiques*, trapped nearly the entire week indoors, turned to them for advice.

Marie knew what her options were for the birth and afterwards. Her main concern was to avoid destitution, for herself and her child. Her choices were very limited and one thing was certain: it was impossible to keep her baby with her and her job, which of course also provided the roof over her head.

In earlier decades, many women in her situation were driven to desperate measures. There was little prospect of support from a society which blamed single mothers for their own misfortune. No such blame attached to men who abandoned women and the babies they had fathered. Some women gave birth alone and in secret, abandoning their baby at birth. Others contemplated abortion, which was illegal and highly dangerous. The most desperate even considered suicide.

By the turn of the century, however, fewer women resorted to such extremes. Social policies and attitudes towards single mothers were changing for the better. This was largely because the population of France was in worrying decline. The state realised something needed to be done. The infant mortality rate remained shockingly high, although it was gradually declining. Moralising in the 19th century gave way to concern for the survival of as many babies as possible. Looking after the poor and pregnant, whether married or single, became a matter of national importance.

The government saw populations of neighbouring nations increasing, including the old enemy Germany. Population growth gave other nations an advantage for industrial expansion and military might. France, by contrast, was falling behind. Babies must be saved for the good of the nation.

Steps introduced around this time included making it easier for mothers to abandon babies, as a last resort, with no questions asked. The aim was to reduce the number of abandoned babies coming to harm before they were found, and cases of infanticide.

Yet tragedies still occurred. Paul Chabot, writing about his grandparents in *Jean et Yvonne, Domestiques en 1900*, records an incident at an apartment block on rue des Batignolles in Paris in 1910. A young *bonne* working there hid her pregnancy and gave birth alone in her attic room. She cut the umbilical cord, wrapped the baby in a sheet and put it in a cupboard, where it was found dead the following morning, after the poor girl failed to report for duty. Rumour was rife in the apartment block that her master was 'far from innocent' in the matter, the implication being he had fathered the child.

Giving a baby up for adoption was still not an option in France in the early 1900s. Only orphans could be adopted, and then only by relatives. If adoption had been possible, few couples would have chosen an illegiti-

3. ON THE BRINK

mate child because of the stigma attached and because of a strong cultural belief that inheritance should only pass along bloodlines. Even so, new mothers leaving hospital were sometimes surreptitiously approached by wealthy couples offering, illegally, to buy their baby.

◆ ◆ ◆ ◆ ◆

At some point, Marie had to pluck up the courage to tell her employers that she was pregnant again. Possibly she confided in her co-worker, the *femme de chambre*, but tried to conceal it from her master and mistress for as long as possible. Even though Marie had kept her job at 4 rue Berger after Henriette was born, she had every reason to be fearful of being sacked this time.

There were no laws to protect *domestiques* who got pregnant, a situation that didn't begin to change until 1909. Marie's employers had no obligation, other than a moral one, to keep her on. Many employers did not want the inconvenience of a pregnant *domestique*. She was unable to work as hard as usual, would need time off to give birth and was distracted by the serious problem of finding childcare. A second pregnancy so soon after the last tested her employer's patience and sympathy.

However, good *cuisinières* were not always easy to find. Marie had already proved she could carry on working after having a baby and her employers may not have wanted to lose her. She had been with the family for some time and perhaps they were fond of her, paternalistic even, considering her almost a member of the family. If she was fortunate, they agreed Marie could continue in her post provided she made arrangements for the baby's care, just as she had for Henriette. Finding childcare was imperative.

Many women in Marie's situation came from the countryside around Paris and turned to their own mother to take their baby. This was not a realistic option for Marie if her family were indeed in the Haute-Savoie. The distance and cost of travel were prohibitive, not to mention the risks to a newborn baby on such a long journey. Besides, the thought of her child growing up hundreds of miles away was distressing. She would not see her for years at a time, or even talk to her. In 1901 telephones had only very recently arrived in Paris, and there were none listed at 4 rue Berger in the directory of the day. It is even less likely people living in remote Alpine villages had a telephone. The only way to keep in touch with home was by letter.

There is little doubt Marie was literate because she dealt with shopping lists and recipes as part of her job. However, her letters home were probably infrequent. For one thing, Marie had little spare time to write and for another, her life was so monotonous and repetitive that there was not much to say beyond 'I am well and still working as a cook at 4 rue Berger'. Of course, her pregnancies were big news to impart, although perhaps she chose not to tell her parents. Living in poverty themselves, Marie knew they could do little to help and she may not have wanted to worry them.

Placing the baby in a nursery was not an option. Nurseries in Paris were few and far between at that time. Even if Marie could afford the fees, they only provided childcare during daytime working hours, which was insufficient for her needs.

Marie could not keep her child with her in the servants' quarters at 4 rue Berger. No employer would tolerate this. However, there were cases of women keeping their baby secretly in their squalid attic room. It was not unheard of in the 19th century for poor working mothers to leave their babies alone all day, attached to a bottle by a dangerously unhygienic cloth comforter to suck on. Until the mother arrived home, there was no one to check they were safe, comfort them, feed them or change their nappy. How any babies managed to survive this degree of neglect is beyond imagining.

Barely less risky was a form of 'childcare' which involved renting the baby out to a professional beggar for ten or fifteen sous a day. Beggars positioned themselves strategically in the shelter of church porches, knowing that with a baby in their arms, passers-by were more likely to take pity and open their purses.

Thankfully, Marie did not have to resort to such extreme measures for her babies. In the early 1900s, there were a number of charitable and public welfare organisations in Paris set up to help poor, pregnant women with the practical challenges they faced.

✦ ✦ ✦ ✦ ✦

Marie continued to work throughout her pregnancy, coping as best she could with the inevitable discomforts. If she was fortunate enough not to suffer from morning sickness, the tiredness of the third trimester was unavoidable. This was exacerbated by the physical demands of her job.

Hopefully, the *femme de chambre* spared Marie from too much lifting and strain. But she still had to climb up and down the stairs several times a day between the apartment and street level, carrying groceries back from

3. ON THE BRINK

the market, and finally up to her bed on the sixth floor when her working day was done.

Marie was at least well-nourished. In Parisian households, most employers allowed the *cuisinière* to prepare enough at each meal to feed the *domestiques* as well as the family. However, she was strictly forbidden to help herself freely to food.

Most masters and mistresses kept a tight rein on the household finances and a close eye on the provisions, watching for signs the *domestiques* were taking more than they were allowed. In the worst cases, stingy employers deliberately restricted their *domestiques* to small portions or even scraps and leftovers. Marie's employers lived in the wealthy 1st arrondissement and as they could afford more than one servant, they could afford to feed them.

Marie was surrounded by food in her neighbourhood. Besides the huge market at Les Halles, the shops on her street included greengrocers, bakeries and wine merchants. Even if she was not well-fed by her employers, she had plenty of opportunities to supplement her diet, particularly if she was friendly with local stall holders who might occasionally slip her extra bread or a piece of cheese or fruit for herself.

Antenatal care for poor women was almost non-existent. At best, Marie attended one check-up with a community midwife during her pregnancy. This was all the state offered, and she needed her employer's permission for time off to attend. Whether she was able to rest in the last few weeks also depended on her employer's benevolence.

By 1901, pregnant women were entitled to a period of paid maternity leave, because it was recognised that in the final stages of pregnancy, rest increased the baby's chances of survival. However, if Marie's employers refused her maternity leave, realistically there was nothing she could do about it, even if the law was on her side. In any case, spending the day alone in her cramped quarters on the sixth floor, contemplating the future, was hardly an attractive proposition. With nowhere else to go, it was preferable to carry on working as best she could, with extra help from the overworked *femme de chambre*. Her belly swelling and growing heavier with each passing day, Marie struggled on, right up until the day she gave birth.

4: Liberté, Égalité, Fraternité

ONE DAY IN June 1901, Marie went into labour. It was time to make her way to the nearest hospital, the Hôtel-Dieu. Marie went alone and almost certainly walked. There was no one to go with her. The *femme de chambre* would not have been permitted to accompany her, because there was too much work to do. Marie's route from rue Berger took her south, crossing a bridge over the Seine, towards Notre-Dame cathedral, on île de la Cité.[6] In normal circumstances, the journey on foot takes around 20 minutes, but her condition slowed her progress, the contractions forcing her to pause from time to time. The warm June weather added to her discomfort.

Main entrance to the Hôtel-Dieu hospital today, barely altered since the early 1900s

The hospital Marie was heading for is the oldest in Paris. Founded in the year 651 by the Bishop Saint-Landry, for many centuries the Hôtel-Dieu was run by the Chapter of Notre Dame cathedral, next to which it

---

6   An island in the middle of the River Seine and the historic heart of Paris, from which the city expanded over centuries to eventually reach its present size.

4: LIBERTÉ, ÉGALITÉ, FRATERNITÉ

is located. Since 1849 it has been administered by Assistance Publique, the state welfare department. After a number of fires destroyed the old buildings, the hospital was rebuilt in 1877. This is the building Marie saw as she approached.

On arrival, she entered the main reception through an archway inscribed with the French national motto: *Liberté, Egalité, Fraternité* (Freedom, Equality, Brotherhood). It is doubtful she paused to consider the irony of this sentiment for women like her. Desk staff asked Marie to confirm she was already in labour; as she answered '*oui*' she was admitted without further question, otherwise she would have been turned away. She was directed to the maternity ward, a short distance away across the river, on the left bank of the Seine. Here, Marie was to receive free maternity care provided by the state for the next nine days.

Hôtel-Dieu maternity annexe (left), 33 Rue de la Bûcherie, c.1900

The maternity ward was in an old building at 33 rue de la Bûcherie, a narrow street running parallel to the river. Built in the late 18th century and originally used as a grain store, it was one of two buildings forming a separate annexe opposite the main hospital. The maternity building was in a dilapidated condition by 1901 and was eventually demolished in 1908.

Today a public garden, square René-Viviani,[7] stands on the site of the maternity ward, next to Shakespeare and Company, a well-known English-language bookshop which opened in 1951. A photo taken in 1900 and a street plan of the same era show the annexe buildings strad-

---

7   Named after the First World War French Prime Minister.

dled opposite sides of rue de la Bûcherie and were linked by an elevated passageway.

It is interesting that Marie chose to have this baby in hospital, although her options were few. Giving birth to Henriette in the attic at 4 rue Berger the previous year had been a grim experience. Besides the poor hygiene, there was no privacy and little chance to rest. The other servants on the *sixième* were coming and going late at night and early in the morning and were less than happy to have their sleep interrupted by a wailing infant. Marie's employers may have insisted she did not give birth a second time on their premises. Only wealthy women could afford the luxury of one of the city's maternity clinics, which offered the highest standards of care available. However, a hospital birth was not a bad option by 1901. It was very different in earlier times.

Before the late 19th century, infections in hospitals were rife. A hospital birth was a hideously dangerous experience, for both mother and child. Doctors, ignorant of the harm they were inflicting, examined one woman after another without washing their hands in between, spreading infection as they went. Overcrowding exacerbated the problem. A century earlier, both before and after giving birth, women at the Hôtel-Dieu were lodged three or four to a bed. Thankfully, by 1901, conditions on maternity wards had significantly improved and increasing numbers of poor women chose to give birth in hospital.

Nonetheless, the care in hospital was still basic by today's standards. Over-stretched doctors were rarely called to attend a delivery unless it took a very serious turn for the worst. Pain relief for childbirth was still non-existent at the Hôtel-Dieu in 1901.

At least Marie knew giving birth in hospital would give her nine days' rest following the birth. By law, mothers were required to stay in hospital with their newborns for this period. The idea was to reduce the likelihood of the mother abandoning her baby, because she would bond with her infant in that time. Statistically, abandonment raised the chance of a child dying in infancy. Another benefit of a hospital birth was the set of free baby clothes and nappies that Assistance Publique provided to new mothers when they were discharged.

❖ ❖ ❖ ❖ ❖

At 11.30 pm on Tuesday 11 June 1901, Marie gave birth to another daughter, exactly one year and one day since the death of Henriette. In contrast to Henriette Yvonne Marie Louise, the new child was given just

4: LIBERTÉ, ÉGALITÉ, FRATERNITÉ

one name: Yvonne. Perhaps after the tragic loss of Henriette, Marie hardly dared hope her new daughter would survive long enough to appreciate extra names. The nursing staff encouraged Marie to breastfeed and discouraged thoughts of abandonment, but otherwise gave her less attention than first-time mothers.

The beds alongside Marie were occupied by many other poor, single women and they shared their stories, their hopes and their fears for the future. Some voiced optimism about raising their child alone. The nurses knew from experience that sooner or later, most of these mothers would be forced to abandon their babies to the care of the state.

In the very next bed to Marie was a 39-year-old woman called Nérée Monard, who lived with her partner Victor Levesque and worked as a *'femme de ménage'* (cleaning lady or housekeeper) to help support the family. Nérée was one of the lucky ones. She was in a settled relationship and had every chance of raising the new addition to the family herself. Marie and Nérée gave birth on the same day and the two women no doubt got to know each other throughout their stay. Perhaps they formed a special bond, because Nérée named her daughter Marie.

Marie's mixed emotions following Yvonne's birth are not hard to imagine. On one hand, her hospital stay was a special time, getting to know her baby daughter, cuddling her, feeding her, soothing her when she cried – memories to hold on to and treasure in the years ahead. On the other hand, Marie was beset with worry about how she was going to provide for herself and her daughter, and the very real prospect that she would not be able to do so. She smiled at the new baby in her arms and cried remembering the child's older sister Henriette, whom Yvonne would never know and Marie would never see again.

As she nursed Yvonne on the bustling maternity ward, she gazed out of the windows at the ancient church of Saint-Julien-le-Pauvre. In the eighteenth century, brief services were held here for the unfortunate twenty-five per cent of patients who died at the Hôtel-Dieu, prior to their burial at the Clamart cemetery south of the River Seine. In the grounds of the church, she saw a huge tree, the oldest in Paris, planted in 1601 and still growing today. The north-facing windows looked out onto rue de la Bûcherie and the adjoining annexe building. This blocked from view Nôtre Dame cathedral, even though it was just a stone's throw away.

On Friday 14 June, while Marie recovered from the birth, three male hospital employees went to the mairie for the 5th arrondissement to register Yvonne's birth. Their names appear on the birth register, testifying that Yvonne had been born to Marie three days earlier. The same employees carried out this task many times a week for single mothers; it was part of their official duties at the hospital. Their names appear again further up the birth records, registering another birth at the hospital on the same day. The name of Yvonne's father does not appear on the birth register.

The law that forbade naming the father unless he was prepared to take parental responsibility had many heart-breaking consequences. Among the Parisian records are a set of twins by the name of Millet (not related to Marie) born in November 1904, a boy named Maurice and a girl called Louise. The birth register only records the name of the twins' father for Maurice. Next to Louise's name it states '*père non dénommé*' (father not named). The father had chosen to acknowledge his son but not the boy's twin sister. This seemingly heartless and sexist decision no doubt arose from a terrible dilemma born of grinding poverty.

It was also Yvonne's fate to be fatherless. The register states that her father is '*non dénommé*'. He had walked away from Marie and his daughter. For the second time in fifteen months, Marie faced the full responsibility and cost of raising a baby alone.

Marie received no visitors during her stay on the maternity ward. No family members or friends came bearing gifts and good wishes to meet her new baby. The hospital record shows Marie was discharged with baby Yvonne on Thursday 20 June 1901. Despite her limited means, and with the odds stacked against her, she was determined to keep her new daughter. Marie would try her hardest to provide for Yvonne, just as she had with Henriette, and pray for her survival.

Marie's first priority on leaving hospital was to apply for welfare payments. She headed for the central office of Assistance Publique which was conveniently situated around the corner from the hospital at number 3 avenue Victoria, just as it still is today.

In 1899, over 50,000 new mothers requested help from Assistance Publique after childbirth, an indication of the levels of poverty among Parisian parents at that time. New mothers going there for help often had to wait several hours with their newborn before they were seen. They had to complete multiple forms and subject themselves to a grilling from the authorities. In most cases, financial help was approved. Three out of every four single mothers received some form of Assistance Publique support in Paris at this time. The unlucky ones sometimes resorted to prostitution for survival, a fate that befell an estimated 2,000 poor women in Paris in 1900. Once granted, the aid from Assistance Publique could take several days to come through, which was terribly distressing for new mothers in dire need.

4: LIBERTÉ, ÉGALITÉ, FRATERNITÉ

Assistance Publique offices, 3 Avenue Victoria, today

Unlike some women, Marie may not have needed welfare payments for immediate survival. If she had been prudent, she had some money set aside to tide her over. Putting some of their wages into a savings account was the only insurance a *domestique* had to cover periods when they couldn't work. It's estimated that in 1900, a *bonne* who was careful could save 300 Francs a year from her wages. As a *cuisinière*, earning around 50 Francs a month, Marie could have saved more.

Marie had a plan. To allow her to continue working and keep a roof over her head, she was going to entrust her baby to the care of a woman out in the countryside. This was the best she could do. It was simply impossible to keep Yvonne with her. Marie hoped, as many poor single mothers did, that one day her circumstances would change and she and her daughter could be together. In the event, Marie only managed to delay abandoning her child. This delay was nonetheless valuable, giving Yvonne a slightly better chance of survival than abandonment at birth.

As archived documents reveal, soon after leaving hospital, probably the same day, Marie left Paris with her tiny baby. Still weak from giving birth nine days earlier and carrying Yvonne in her arms, she made her way to the Gare du Nord railway station. Here, she handed over 8 Francs for a ticket and boarded a steam train heading 160 kilometres north-west to the small town of Albert, in the department of the Somme. Holding

Yvonne tight, she found a place on one of the hard wooden seats in a third class carriage, cushioned only by the folds of her well-worn skirts. Acrid smoke from the engine caught in her throat as the train departed, and she hugged her baby closer. It was a journey she had made before.

Gare du Nord c.1900

Part Two: Infancy in Thiepval, June 1901 – January 1905

5: The Childminder

THE WOMAN MARIE chose to look after Yvonne is referred to in the records sometimes as an '*éleveuse d'enfants*', sometimes as a '*nourrice*'. The literal translation of '*éleveuse d'enfants*' is 'raiser of children'. A '*nourrice*' was a woman who literally fed (or nourished) a baby. Historically, and most commonly, a '*nourrice*' was a wet nurse, who breastfed another woman's baby after she had herself given birth.

In other words, Marie had found a childminder who would take Yvonne into her home and look after her there, freeing her to work. Her poverty forced her to outsource motherhood; however, the arrangement was not at all unusual. There was a long tradition of Parisian mothers of all social classes, not just the poor, sending their newborns to a *nourrice* in the countryside. Wealthy mothers often preferred to avoid the inconvenience of breastfeeding and the disruption to their busy social lives it entailed. They also reasoned the clean country air was better for their baby than the polluted air of Paris.

Others hired a *nourrice* from the countryside to breastfeed their baby at home in the city. The *nourrice* left her own baby behind in the countryside to be bottle-fed by her family. The female French Impressionist painter Berthe Morisot, from a wealthy Parisian family, is an example of how this custom worked. Morisot painted her own baby daughter being suckled by Angele, the wet nurse she employed (*La nourrice Angele allaitant Julie Manet*, 1880). It is a poignant and conflicted image. On the one hand, Morisot was blazing a trail for female artists in a male-dominated world and putting a working-class woman centre-stage in a painting. On the other hand, poverty had compelled Angele to live apart from her own baby to earn money feeding Morisot's child Julie.

For Marie, whose life was circumscribed by poverty, engaging the services of a *nourrice* was not a matter of choice, but of necessity. Most babies born to Parisian *domestiques* were taken to a *nourrice* in the countryside. The majority had been abandoned at birth by their desperately poor mothers and were in the care of the state, which placed them in rural

5: THE CHILDMINDER

foster homes. The rest were the children of women like Marie who were trying their hardest to support their baby themselves.

The Parisian authorities had no facilities for babies of the poor to be looked after in the city. The official view was children would be healthier if raised in the country and grow up better behaved, away from the corrupting influences of the city. With an exodus of young people heading from their childhood villages to cities in search of better jobs and wages, it was also a useful policy for repopulating the countryside. The decline in the agricultural workforce across France was a serious concern, threatening the nation's food production.

Records show the *nourrice* Marie chose was the same woman who had looked after Henriette during her short life. On the face of it, her decision is surprising, given Henriette died in her care. The name of the *nourrice* was Victorine Talon and she lived in Thiepval, a very small village not far from Albert. When Marie realised another baby was on the way, it was pragmatic to write to Victorine and ask her to help again. Even if Marie had reservations, she worked very long hours and had little time or energy to devote to finding childcare.

Although Marie evidently did not blame Victorine for Henriette's death, she was acutely aware of the risks for Yvonne in this arrangement. Babies frequently died in the care of a *nourrice*. In 1900, a third of all abandoned babies placed by the state with a *nourrice* died before their first birthday, three times higher than the average infant mortality rate. A hundred years earlier, as many as three-quarters died. The appalling mortality rate among babies in the care of *nourrices* was the result of poor living conditions, malnutrition, disease and a lack of knowledge of the importance of good hygiene.

Marie's childcare arrangements were determined by what she could afford and this gave her very little choice. Many single mothers struggled to pay even for this perilous care without some help from Assistance Publique. The basic cost of a *nourrice* was in the region of 25 Francs a month, around half Marie's wages. She was entitled to support from the state covering the cost of transport to the *nourrice*, the first ten months' payments to her and essential clothes for the baby. After this, the expense of Yvonne's care would fall completely to Marie. The ongoing financial commitment made her difficult existence increasingly more precarious. It was now almost impossible for Marie to save any money as a buffer against further unexpected events and misfortune. Her wages would have to stretch further and further as Yvonne grew and her savings shrank to nothing.

Victorine was an approved *nourrice* with plenty of experience. The authorities vetted all *nourrices* and archived documents include the two certificates Victorine required to work. One was signed by a doctor and the other by the mayor of Thiepval. To obtain the mayor's certificate, Victorine confirmed that her 'husband' had consented to her working as a *nourrice*, and that she had a crib and a fire guard.

There were rules governing *nourrices*, introduced in the 19th century under a programme to reduce infant mortality. Victorine had to 'keep the baby very clean, whether the baby is healthy or unwell', and in particular must 'not let the baby sleep in the bed with her, nor allow any domestic animals including dogs, cats or pigs in the same room as the crib, nor place the light too close to the crib'. The light in question was a naked flame, either an oil lamp or a candle, and the risk of serious burns very real. It seems amusing by 21st-century standards that someone responsible for raising a child had to be told to keep pigs out of the room where the baby slept. But in 19th-century rural France, animals were regularly allowed to wander into the home, particularly in winter and when fuel was scarce. They helped to keep the place warm. There were recorded incidents of babies being bitten by pigs, sometimes fatally.

Failure to abide by the rules, or neglect of a child, could result in serious charges, punishable by a prison sentence of between three months to two years, plus a fine of 50 Francs and six centimes. With *nourrices* sometimes motivated only by money, the threat of punishment for maltreatment was a necessary attempt to ensure adequate standards of care. In reality, however, record-keeping was poor and it was difficult for the authorities to monitor *nourrices* effectively.

Census information shows that Victorine's 'husband' was Adolphe Thuillier who worked as an agricultural day labourer (*'ouvrier'* or *'journalier'*). Adolphe was twelve years older than Victorine. The couple lived alone in a cottage on rue de Pozières, one of two roads that cross at the heart of Thiepval. Although it was one of the main thoroughfares through the village, it was no more than a quiet lane leading to the neighbouring village of Pozières.

Victorine and Adolphe were not married. Many couples cohabited rather than marrying because they couldn't afford the cost of all the paperwork marriage involved in those days. In 1901, Victorine was 50 years old and Adolphe was aged 62. As a day labourer, Adolphe did not have regular employment. After a lifetime of labouring outdoors, his physical strength was inevitably diminished. There was nonetheless still some work avail-

5: THE CHILDMINDER

able for him, at least in the growing season, since many of Thiepval's younger, fitter men had left to find better-paid work in towns and cities.

Each morning, he pulled on clothes typical for agricultural labourers at that time. He wore an old loose-fitting shirt tucked into dun-coloured baggy trousers, belted at the waist. Over this he wore a waistcoat, adding a well-worn jacket in winter. His work garments were rarely washed and bore signs of Victorine's mending stretching back years. Putting on a flat cap as protection against the elements, he set off to present himself at the gates of farms to ask if help was needed. There were times throughout the year when there was no work, especially in the winter months when the fields lay dormant. So the income Victorine earned looking after the babies of the Parisian poor was much-needed, even if the job was not well-paid. Women resorted to this work only when there were no other options. This was often the case in poor rural areas and the Somme countryside was no exception. *Nourrices* had a very low status. It was very poorly paid compared to factory or shop work. The mayor's certificate states Victorine was reliant on her husband's wages, implying there was no other employment open to her.

Fifty-year-old Victorine was going to bottle-feed Yvonne and had never been a wet nurse. The certificate shows she was not herself a mother and had bottle-fed all the babies she looked after. Adolphe, however, had a son, Achille, by his first 'wife' Zulma Morel. She died in 1870 when their son was just six years old. He can be found aged 17 living with his father and Victorine on the 1881 Thiepval census but by 1901 he had left home.

The certificates reveal much about Victorine. She had previously looked after nineteen infants over a period of twenty years. Henriette had been the last of these. The certificate doesn't name Henriette but states the last child in Victorine's care had died of internal convulsions 12 months previously, on 10 June 1900. The death register for Thiepval reveals a baby called Henriette Yvonne Marie Louise Millet died on that date, the only death in the village that day. Without doubt, Henriette was the child referred to on Victorine's certificate.

Henriette was almost certainly not the only baby to have perished in Victorine's care. Her death perhaps hit her particularly hard because afterwards, she let her authorisations lapse, and accepted no more children until Yvonne arrived a year later.

The doctor's certificate, completed by Dr Pierre Toussaint in Albert on 7 March 1901, describes Victorine. She was an unprepossessing woman with mousy hair, a full face, pale complexion, low brow, strong nose, dark grey eyes, an 'average' mouth, a round chin and 'no distinguishing marks'.

The mayor's certificate states that she lived a 'good and moral' life, her habits and routines conforming to local customs. Victorine lived quietly and did not draw attention.

Although Victorine obtained the doctor's certificate in good time, it seems she only remembered the mayor's certificate at the last minute. It is dated 20 June 1901 – the day Marie and Yvonne left hospital. This, and Marie's pressing need to get back to work, point to her leaving Paris with Yvonne the same day. Unable to take the baby back to her attic room, Marie had nowhere else to go.

Victorine hurried to the mairie, just along the road from her home on rue de Pozières, to complete the documentation. She wanted to be at the station in Albert when Marie and the new baby arrived. Remembering their meeting the previous year, when Marie handed Henriette into her care, gave her butterflies in her stomach. The responsibility of looking after another Millet baby after the death of the last was daunting. Yet Victorine and Adolphe needed the money and it was clear Marie harboured no blame.

✦ ✦ ✦ ✦ ✦

Albert station, early 1900s

As the train puffed slowly into Albert station that summer's day in 1901, Marie scanned the platform for Victorine. Her heart lurched when she spotted her quietly approaching. Victorine helped Marie as she climbed

5: THE CHILDMINDER

down from the carriage cradling the baby in her arms. Victorine chose her words of greeting carefully, expressing her sorrow at Henriette's loss and the bonniness of her newborn younger sister.

Marie yearned to take Yvonne all the way to Thiepval herself. She would have liked to gather flowers to lay on Henriette's grave, marked in the churchyard with a simple wooden cross, already weathered and fading. But she had neither time nor energy to walk all the way to Thiepval and back to Albert, a round-trip of 16 kilometres. It was too much so soon after giving birth. Nor could she easily spare the fare for a horse-drawn cab. The last thing Marie did before parting with her daughter was to feed her, perhaps in a quiet corner of the red-brick station waiting room. She kissed her tenderly, tears spilling over, before allowing Victorine to take Yvonne gently from her.

Feeling very lonely, Marie caught the next train back to Paris. The return journey seemed interminable. Other passengers sensed the distress of the young woman in their third class carriage and smiled at her sympathetically. From her demeanour and appearance, they could guess her situation, which was all too common. She fought back tears and became increasingly uncomfortable as her body continued to produce milk for her baby. The need to start working again weighed heavily on her mind.

No record exists to say whether or not she returned to her old job at 4 rue Berger. Even if her employers agreed to take her back, she may have chosen to try her luck elsewhere if Yvonne's father lived there. As a *cuisinière*, her services were in demand in Paris. But she still needed a reference from her previous employers to get another job. For many women leaving a position in Marie's circumstances, a reference was not forthcoming. Two pregnancies in quick succession would not warrant a good reference for a *cuisinière*. However, by law employers were forbidden to provide a bad reference, which could condemn a *domestique* to destitution.

After an emotional and exhausting day, Marie arrived back at Gare du Nord. If she was not returning to her old job, she faced an urgent need to find work. A sou would buy the day's edition of *Le Petit Parisien* newspaper, whose small ads included several that read '*on demande bonne cuisinière*' ('we need a good cook'). Having nowhere to live would force her to follow up vacancies immediately. It's possible she had nowhere to spend the night and forked out money she could ill afford on a cheap hotel room.

❖ ❖ ❖ ❖ ❖

Meanwhile, Victorine returned to Thiepval with her tiny new charge. A horse-drawn cab cost money and if Marie had given her the fare for the one-way journey, it was tempting to pocket this and return home on foot. It was eight kilometres to Thiepval. She could carry the sleeping Yvonne strapped to her back, and the small bundle Marie had given her containing clothing and nappies was only light. She rested in Aveluy and Authuille, the villages she passed through on her way.

Thiepval c.1900

Victorine's home on rue de Pozières was a simple country cottage, of the type that can be seen in photos of Thiepval taken before the Great War. These were built in the late 19th century, when better housing materials became more widely available and could be transported on the new rail networks. They replaced hovels built of timber with thatched roofs and dirt floors which housed not only people, but farm animals and assorted vermin too. The newer homes, though an improvement, were still very basic, dimly lit and sparsely furnished.

The fireplace or stove was the heart of the home, providing warmth and somewhere to cook, although the lack of ventilation made the interior smoky and added to the grime from insufficient sanitation and the mud of the countryside. However, it was superior to Marie's own grim living quarters and it is clear from Victorine's certification that her home was judged to be well-kept. It was orderly, adequately furnished and as clean as would normally be expected in a home of that kind.

Roof tiles on a number of homes were still being replaced when Yvonne

5: THE CHILDMINDER

first arrived in Thiepval, following a tornado and violent hailstorm that had swept through the village on 1 June, causing minor damage. The storm foreshadowed devastation of a very different magnitude that would strike Thiepval thirteen years later.

Thiepval sits high above the lush valley of the River Ancre in Picardy, with commanding views over the countryside. In times of conflict, it is a prime defensive position. During the 1914-18 war, the Germans would occupy Thiepval almost from the start of the conflict. Many villagers fled as the enemy approached. Men of fighting age had already left to join the French army. Those remaining soon discovered that among numerous humiliations and privations forced on them, they must pay 'war contributions' to the Germans. Soldiers then 'bought' food and supplies from the villagers with the villagers' own money. It was not long before every last resident had gone from Thiepval, including Victorine, Adolphe and any children in their care.

Soon the village was riddled with tunnels and trenches as the Germans turned it into a stronghold. They held Thiepval for two years until the Allies regained it during the Battle of the Somme. As the fighting intensified, any last trace of the peaceful pre-war village was utterly obliterated and the surrounding countryside decimated. A British journalist, watching events unfold from behind the lines, described seeing 500 shells raining down on Thiepval in less than half an hour. The ground on which the village had stood was eventually liberated by the British Army on 27 September 1916. But that was not the end of it. Thiepval was retaken by the Germans in the spring of 1918 before once more being liberated by the Allies, for the final time, in August 1918.

Only five of Thiepval's original residents ever returned when, several years after the Armistice, reconstruction got underway. The war had utterly destroyed an entire community and way of life. Nothing remained from the place where Yvonne spent her infancy. More than a century later, the war lies heavy on the landscape still. Serried ranks of tombstones stand to attention in military cemeteries dotted around the area. At Thiepval itself the gigantic Thiepval Memorial, designed by world-renowned architect Sir Edward Lutyens, commemorates the tens of thousands of soldiers who fought on the Somme and whose bodies were never found.

❖ ❖ ❖ ❖ ❖

Such total destruction was unimaginable when Yvonne arrived in Thiepval as a newborn baby in June 1901. It was a peaceful, thriving village with around 200 inhabitants living in 60 houses surrounded by farm land. There was a church, a school, a *café-tabac* and a *sucrerie* (sugar refinery). Sugar beet was grown on an industrial scale in the surrounding fields. The local farmers also grew wheat, oats, barley, and rye, and made cider and honey.

A large château dominated the village, where Count Jacques de Bréda and his family lived. The château provided much of the local employment and was also a source of charitable support for the villagers. In the tradition of *'noblesse oblige'*, the Count and Countess regarded it their duty to be kind and generous to those less fortunate, particularly in times of real hardship. The Countess quietly visited the sick and the hungry in Thiepval, dispensing nourishing *pot-au-feu* (beef stew) during the depths of winter. Her benevolence extended to looked-after children like Yvonne who might receive gifts of extra clothing or a warm baby blanket.

When Victorine eventually entered her cottage on arriving back from Albert, feeding Yvonne was her first priority. It was essential the baby took quickly to the bottle. Victorine's certificates specifically authorised her to accept an unweaned infant for bottle-feeding. For Marie, a bottle-feeding service was cheaper than a wet nurse, and more reliable. By 1901 bottle feeding was comparatively safe. Sterilised milk, even infant formulas, were now available and bottles were made from glass or metal. Until the late 19th century, before the links between cleanliness, bacteria and disease began to be properly understood, bottle feeding had been highly dangerous. Babies were fed from wooden bottles which harboured all kinds of germs.

Bottle-feeding was also more likely to provide Yvonne with good nutrition because wet nurses were not always truthful. Sometimes they did not breastfeed the babies in their charge at all, mixing their own dubious formula milk instead. They did this either to save the time and energy of breastfeeding or because they were insufficiently nourished themselves to produce enough milk, particularly if they were also feeding their own baby. It was only the higher-paid wet nurses to the wealthy who could be relied on.

Babies entrusted to Victorine earlier in her twenty-year career were fortunate to survive the ordeal of bottle-feeding. However, even if most had died, the authorities were not concerned about Victorine's suitability based on this statistic alone. Before the late 19th century, it was a case of survival of the fittest and it was accepted as normal that many babies would not survive. Victorine's intentions were not in doubt and her standards of care were the norm for that time.

5: THE CHILDMINDER

Victorine was well-known in the tight-knit community. Census information shows both she and Adolphe had been born and raised in the village and came from established Thiepval families. Victorine was sufficiently trusted by the village mayor to be allowed to continue working as a *nourrice*. Signing her medical certificate, Dr Toussaint confirmed that she 'fulfilled the desirable conditions to raise a bottle-fed baby'.

Marie showed great trust in Victorine, handing over another precious daughter to her care. Victorine was as diligent as she could be caring for Yvonne. After what had happened to her older sister, any sign of illness caused Victorine great anxiety. She nursed Yvonne through inevitable colds and fevers, and kept her warm, safe and fed. Weeks and months passed, stretching into years. Life was uneventful in the tranquillity of the Somme countryside, the daily routine varying only with the seasons. Settled by the rhythm and regularity of the days, baby Yvonne thrived under Victorine's watchful eye.

Marie tried to stay in touch with Yvonne, if only by notes to Victorine, enquiring after her daughter's progress, enclosed with the monthly payments. There was a reliable postal service from Albert, although Victorine and Adolphe, poor country folk, may have only had basic literacy. With no telephone, communications were difficult. Perhaps Marie sent small gifts and keepsakes for Yvonne, the only way she could express her love to her child. She visited whenever she could, which was rarely, if at all. With no holiday entitlement, she had to ask for a whole day off work to make the return journey, and it was a struggle to pay the train fare.

As Yvonne grew, she would barely know her mother, believing Maman Talon and Papa Thuillier were her parents. It was Victorine and Adolphe who were there when Yvonne cut her first tooth, said her first word and took her first step, not Marie. Yvonne would cling shyly to Victorine's skirts when Marie paid a visit after an absence of many months. Marie was heartbroken to see her child's reluctance to come to her when she opened her arms. Over time, and as her finances became more strained, the hope she could ever fulfil her role as a mother gradually faded. Her resolve to hold onto her daughter began to weaken.

6: Innocence

Yvonne's early childhood was normal enough in the home of Victorine and Adolphe. There is no reason to suppose they were other than gentle people who did their best for her within their restricted means. Like most people in rural areas, they were living in great poverty. The payments from Marie were their only reliable source of income.

Their diet was limited. Bread was the mainstay, eaten with soup made from the vegetables they grew in their potager (kitchen garden), on a small patch of land behind the cottage. Chestnuts gathered in the woods and roasted over the fire made a filling meal in winter. Occasionally, Adolphe snared a rabbit for dinner or hooked a fish in the River Ancre, but otherwise meat of any kind was a rare luxury. Living in northern France, an abundant dairy farming region, they bought milk, cheese and, when they could afford it, cream. The honey produced on local farms was a treat for special occasions.

There was no plumbing in the cottage. Households drew their water in buckets from the village pump or well which provided a safe, clean supply for drinking. Cleanliness and hygiene in the home were very difficult to maintain and were not high priorities at that time. Scientists had only recently made the connection between harmful bacteria and disease, and this knowledge had yet to fully permeate the way ordinary people lived day-to-day.

For Victorine and Adolphe, like peasants all over the French countryside, water was a precious commodity. Little could be spared for cleaning or personal hygiene. People bathed infrequently and for babies, bathing was even believed to be unhealthy. Dealing with dirty nappies presented great difficulties and mothers had to be pragmatic. Nappies might be scraped and dried off in the sun but seldom washed. In the summer, infants were left naked from the waist down until they were toilet trained.

Doing the laundry was a communal activity. On wash days Victorine carried Yvonne on her hip and a bundle of laundry on her head to the '*lavoir*' (wash house). It was a walk of two and a half kilometres to reach the *lavoir*, beside the River Ancre, in the neighbouring hamlet of Saint-Pièrre Division. The women kept each other company as they dunked,

6: INNOCENCE

swirled and scrubbed linens in the cold river water, while the children played contentedly on the shallow banks nearby.

Saint-Pièrre Divion, 1912
Courtesy of: Amiens, Société des Antiquaires de Picardie (en dépôt aux Arch. dép. de la Somme) 14FI 33/46

Babies living in these basic conditions were vulnerable to a range of illnesses and health problems. Had Yvonne been in state care at this time, a doctor sent by Assistance Publique would have checked her health regularly and vaccinated her against common illnesses. Vaccination was a relatively new public health measure. Tetanus and diphtheria were among the first vaccines introduced, having been developed during the 1890s. In the event, Yvonne may never have been examined by a doctor before the age of three and a half. Marie almost certainly had no spare money for medical care. If Yvonne fell ill, Victorine, like other *nourrices*, resorted to homemade remedies, some of them highly dubious. One recorded 'remedy' for painful teething was to rub the infant's gums with hare brain. Thankfully, Yvonne was a robust child. Marie had given her a good start. Being well-nourished herself suggests she carried her baby to full term and successfully breastfed her during those first precious nine days of life. In Victorine's care, she grew to be healthy and strong, even though living in rural poverty.

Despite the risks, the clean air of the beautiful rolling countryside and plenty of outdoors play were far better for her than the smoke and grime of Paris. Women in the village kept an eye on young children playing outside in the dirt, Yvonne among them, chasing chickens and splashing barefoot in puddles. Victorine struggled to clothe the growing child on the income she received from Marie and had to be resourceful. Any serviceable clothes she had kept, outgrown by previous children in her care, she patched and mended to extend their life. Yvonne had no more than two outfits, a simple cotton smock dress for summer and a woollen one for winter. Shoes, if she ever wore them, were little wooden clogs or second-hand leather boots.

Yvonne had very few toys apart from perhaps a simple rag doll made by Victorine. Little children are, of course, just as happy playing with a wooden spoon and a pan. Yvonne could sit on the floor of the cottage happily mimicking Victorine's actions as she stirred a pot at the stove. As soon as Yvonne was old enough, Victorine taught her to help with very simple chores, perhaps shelling peas or passing pegs as she hung laundry out to dry in the breeze. Life was hard in rural France and it was necessary for children to contribute to the running of the home, even from a young age. Yvonne's daily life was little different to any other young child in Thiepval and her situation was not unique. There were undoubtedly other children being raised by a *nourrice* in the village.

Yvonne's first few years were settled and stable among this close-knit rural community. Then suddenly her small world and everything she knew were turned completely upside down.

7: A Mother's Desperation

IN JANUARY 1905 Yvonne's familiar life with her *nourrice* Victorine ended abruptly. Aged just three and a half, she was taken into the care of the Assistance Publique. The record states, 'the young girl Yvonne Millet was found in a state of abandon following the disappearance of her mother'. Although this description conjures up an image of her wandering alone in the street, this was not the case.

By the early 1900s, there was no need for anyone to abandon a child in this way. Welfare measures were in place to make it easy for women to abandon children, with few questions asked; such was the scale of abandonment due to poverty. It would have been completely illogical, not to mention extremely cruel and against the law, to take Yvonne somewhere outside and leave her there alone. The villagers knew her. If she was found on her own, a neighbour would have returned her to Victorine's cottage.

The official description of the circumstances was a technicality, allowing Victorine to relinquish responsibility for Yvonne and pass her into the care of the department of the Somme. Documents on Yvonne's file indicate Victorine went into the mairie in Thiepval, on Thursday 5 January, to seek help. She no doubt explained she hadn't heard from Marie or been paid by her in some time and could no longer look after Yvonne.

In a village as small as Thiepval, the mayor, probably a local farmer, knew the residents well, including Victorine's family. Born in the village, she was the oldest of Jean-Baptiste Talon and Augustine Carpentier's five children. She had worked as a *nourrice* in the village for more than twenty years. He knew Victorine and Adolphe were very poor and understood their predicament perfectly.

Victorine had no choice other than to hand Yvonne over to the care of the state. She could not afford to keep her without being paid. The same day, the mayor wrote a letter to the Somme departmental authorities asking for arrangements to be made to take Yvonne into their care. Victorine told the authorities everything she knew about Yvonne, including her date and place of birth, and her mother's name, which were duly recorded. Then there was a pause while the wheels of bureaucracy turned. First, the authorities searched for Marie, starting with her last known address in Paris. After Yvonne's birth, she may have moved on from 4 rue Berger and whatever address Victorine was able to provide, they failed to find Marie there. The people they spoke to either didn't know, or did not want to reveal, where she had gone.

As part of the process, the authorities needed to categorise Yvonne's case, choosing from three categories laid down by law. The first was 'children found in a public place, parents unknown' and the second was 'orphans'. The third was 'morally abandoned children', whose parents had neglected them to the extent of abandonment, the whereabouts of the parents unknown. Yvonne's case was assigned to this third category. The definition of 'moral abandonment' suggests wilful neglect. In reality, for many poor single mothers like Marie, their situation was desperate.

It is impossible to know exactly what happened leading up to this pivotal event in Yvonne's life; however, there are several possibilities. Her situation was certainly not unique. The most common form of abandonment of toddlers and young children was direct from the *nourrice* when payments from the mother had stopped. No matter how fond of Yvonne they had become, Victorine and Adolphe were too poor to look after her without being paid.

Adolphe was by now 66 years old and the decades of manual toil had taken their toll. Victorine's wages were ever more important to their existence. Distressing though it was, Victorine needed to tell the authorities quickly once the payments from Marie ceased. She and Adolphe now had a serious gap in their income. By the time of the following year's census in Thiepval, they were again making ends meet. The Count de Breda had given Adolphe some work at the château, probably an act of charity to an old man who had lived his whole life in Thiepval. Victorine was looking after two more children from Paris, a boy and a girl.

Marie may have disappeared on purpose, her circumstances unchanged since Yvonne was born and her hope diminished. Her period of entitlement to welfare payments had long since ended and her savings had dwindled to nothing. She remained too poor to take Yvonne back. Still in domestic service, she had no prospect of providing a home to raise her daughter.

More than three years after Yvonne's birth, the continuing cost of paying Victorine's wages caused Marie severe hardship. To make matters worse, the cost was increasing as Yvonne grew. It left Marie with very little spare money to buy even the essentials for herself and it was impossible to put any money aside as a safety net. With her life still shackled to never-end-

7: A MOTHER'S DESPERATION

ing work with no imaginable way out, her resolve to provide for Yvonne probably began to weaken. Her daughter barely knew her.

❖ ❖ ❖ ❖ ❖

Marie's endless struggle to provide for Yvonne made her own life at times seem barely worth living. While the other *sixièmes* grabbed whatever diversions were open to them in their meagre time off, Marie's overstretched finances meant she missed out. By 1905, *domestiques* were flocking to a hugely successful new form of entertainment most of them could afford: the cinema.

It is easy to understand how popular cinemas were with people on low wages. For an entrance fee of around 1 Franc, people trapped in domestic service were briefly transported from the harsh realities of their lives into a fantasy world. The cinema was booming in Paris at this time. It was a French invention. The word 'cinema' derives from '*cinematographe*', the camera-projector instrument made by two entrepreneurial brothers from Lyon, Auguste and Louis Lumière. Other early French film pioneers included Charles and Emile Pathé and Léon Gaumont.

However, it was the Lumière brothers who screened the first-ever motion picture to the paying public, on 28 December 1895, at the Grand Café on boulevard des Capucines, Paris. The audience was captivated by ten short silent films, directed by Louis Lumière, depicting everyday French life. First on the bill was *Workers Leaving the Lumière Factory*, believed to be the first true motion picture. Other films featured a gardener using a sprinkler, Auguste Lumière having breakfast with his wife and his daughter Andrée, and another of Andrée trying to catch goldfish in a bowl.

There were around one hundred cinemas in Paris by the mid-1900s, typically seating up to three hundred people and showing programmes of short films, each around ten or fifteen minutes long. The films of George Méliès, a director who specialised in special effects and illusions, drew huge audiences. If Marie ever saw his most famous film, the 1902 science fiction hit *Le voyage dans la lune* (*A trip to the moon*), her continuing poverty and servitude soon brought her back down to earth.

❖ ❖ ❖ ❖ ❖

Given her own terrible hardship, it is unsurprising if Marie gave up on her dream of a future where her daughter could be with her. With huge sadness and reluctance, she concluded it was best to walk away from Yvonne. She knew the state would step in and provide for her more successfully than she could.

Her decision may have been driven by pressure from Victorine to pay her more money. Yvonne had stayed in Victorine's care longer than infants normally stayed with a *nourrice*, most moving on as soon as they were weaned, or by the age of two at the latest. Yvonne, aged three and a half, was becoming increasingly expensive to feed and clothe. However, it seems her age was not in itself an issue for Victorine. By the time of the 1911 census, she was looking after two *enfants de l'Assistance* placed with her by the state, one a baby and the other thirteen years old. The problem was simply that Marie couldn't afford another centime more than she was already paying.

Unemployment could be another reason Marie let Yvonne go. There was no state welfare support for those without work. Life as a *domestique* was very insecure, with dismissal possible at any time on a whim, for the slightest thing. *Domestiques* had no rights or protections and the only place they could turn to for help was the church, for whatever charity could be found there. Since there were plenty of positions for good *cuisinières* in Paris, if Marie did lose her job and was unable to find another, it was probably due to ill-health.

Tuberculosis in particular was rife among *domestiques* in Paris due to the insanitary conditions in which they lived. Doctors were beginning to raise serious concerns about this by the start of the 20th century. In France alone, the disease was claiming around 150,000 lives a year, which one doctor compared to wiping out a town the size of Toulouse annually.

In October 1905, in an effort to tackle the problem, experts from across the globe came together in Paris for an international congress on tuberculosis. To coincide with this, there was a major exhibition at the Grand Palais to raise public awareness and showcase new scientific approaches to tackling the disease. There, two photos were shown side by side: one was a faithful reproduction of a *domestique*'s sixth-floor room in the Champs-Elysée district of the fashionable 8th arrondissement, and the other was an image of a prison cell at Fresnes. The cell was habitable and healthy, the *domestique*'s room was not.

The true reason Marie let go of Yvonne is lost in the mists of time. There is nothing in the archive records to shed light on what actually happened. Marie almost certainly remained in domestic service in Paris, where the best-paid jobs were to be found. When she vanished from Yvonne's life, it was not because of another baby or because she had married or had died – at least, not in Paris. Her name cannot be found in the registers of

7: A MOTHER'S DESPERATION

births, marriages or deaths for the whole of Paris between 1903 to 1912. If she had returned home to Annecy (if indeed she was from there), she does not appear in the birth, marriage or death records for this period there either.

Desperation is the most likely reason Marie abandoned Yvonne, a last resort in dire circumstances. She loved Yvonne, although the long separation inevitably loosened the maternal bond. By 1905, the prolonged absences meant Marie barely knew her daughter. The emotional wrench she felt, though deeply painful, was less profound than if she had raised Yvonne herself up to that point.

Marie's agony was less acute than for women forced to give up their child directly from their own care. Poignant records from the same era, in the archives at the Foundling Hospital in London, testify to the suffering of mothers who took their child there. Before parting with their child, many cut two small squares from the fabric of their clothing. One was for themselves, the other was kept on the child's file. The two matching fabric squares could in theory be used to help identify the child if ever the mother came back for them. The mothers pinned a note to the square for the hospital file, pouring out in words and drawings their love, anguish and hope that one day they would reclaim their child. Sadly, only one per cent of mothers were ever able to do so.

The situation was little different in France. Marie knew how difficult it would be to reclaim Yvonne in the future. The state demanded that before a mother could reclaim her child, she must satisfy five criteria. These included being married and repaying all of the state's costs for looking after her child. As every year passed, the cost of reclaiming Yvonne would increase and the possibility of doing so would diminish. Marie knew the separation was going to be permanent.

The death of Henriette and letting go of Yvonne were sorrows Marie bore for the rest of her life. We don't know if she ever went on to have more children. She cherished the memory of carrying each of her baby girls for nine months and snuggling them close as newborns in her arms. She thought often of her precious, rare visits to Thiepval, marvelling at how much Yvonne had grown. Yet such memories were tainted with sorrow as her daughter grew away from her, not understanding who she was. In 1901 Marie had hoped leaving Yvonne with Victorine would be a temporary measure. By early 1905, Marie realised it was not to be.

There is no doubt Marie suffered as a result of her heart-rending decision. Yet Yvonne's suffering was even more severe. She lived her whole life with a profound sense of rejection, never knowing her mother had loved her and never knowing who her father was. There was a huge void at her core.

* * * * *

Whatever led up to Yvonne's abandonment, on Tuesday 31 January 1905, the paperwork was completed, and she was officially taken into state care. A social worker came to collect her from the cottage on rue de Pozières. Victorine hugged little Yvonne as she said farewell, fixing a smile to her face that belied her feelings. Yvonne was now an *'enfant de l'Assistance'* – a child in the care of Assistance Publique.

From Thiepval Yvonne was taken to Amiens, the capital of the Somme department, 42 kilometres to the south-west. At first, the day seemed like a big adventure for the small child, although she was shy in the company of a complete stranger, probably a social worker from Assistance Publique. The first leg of the journey was by horse-drawn cab to Albert railway station. Yvonne was too young to walk the eight kilometres from Thiepval and too old to be carried all that way. The driver stopped outside the station and the social worker lifted Yvonne down, telling her they were going to catch a train and making it sound like something to feel excited about.

Yet at first, the huge, noisy steam train frightened Yvonne. It was her very first train journey. As it chugged out of Albert, she knelt beside the social worker on the wooden seat to watch as the town and then the countryside sped past. The novelty distracted her from her confusion about what was happening on this strange day. Eventually, the train pulled into Amiens.

Leaving the bustling station, Yvonne was wide-eyed and startled at the huge buildings, busy streets and noisy trams clattering past. The contrast of the big city with the tiny village Yvonne had left behind overwhelmed her senses. Holding the social worker's hand tightly, she began to walk. They skirted the city centre with its huge gothic cathedral and headed directly to their destination, the Hospice Saint-Charles on boulevard Maignan Larivière. It was a distance of just over one kilometre.

Yvonne's route took her past the home of Jules Vernes, the famous author of *Journey to the Centre of the Earth*, *Twenty Thousand Leagues Under the Sea* and *Around the World in Eighty Days*. He lived and wrote at 44 boulevard Longueville (now boulevard Jules-Verne). In January 1905, when Yvonne passed by on her way to the hospice, he was in his final days. He died in Amiens in March 1905 at the age of seventy-seven.

7: A MOTHER'S DESPERATION

Hospice Saint-Charles was an institution of the state care system in the Somme. The headquarters of Assistance Publique for the department of the Somme was based here. There were similar hospices right across France, taking care of vulnerable people of all ages who were too infirm or disabled to look after themselves, together with orphaned and abandoned children. The hospice in Amiens had a long history. Established by the Catholic church, it first opened in 1770, and continued to provide shelter and sustenance for those in need until 1968.

Former Hospice Saint-Charles, Amiens, today part of the University of Picardy

Photos in the Somme Archives collection, taken between 1900 and 1910, give a glimpse of hospice life during the era of Yvonne's arrival. They include portraits of nuns, wearing the distinctive habits and wimples of the *Filles de la Charité de Saint Vincent de Paul* (Daughters of the Charity of Saint Vincent de Paul). This order ran the hospice with the help of *domestiques* and other staff.

One photo shows a scene in the kitchen, where a nun stands with a weary-looking *bonne* of indeterminate age. Working in a hospice was one of the least attractive and most poorly paid positions open to a *domestique*. Another photo was taken in what appears to be a ward for the elderly. The hospice was very institutional, well-ordered but sparse. Conditions in hospices had improved in recent years and the accommodation was simple and clean, although not offering much comfort.

*The kitchen at Hospice Saint-Charles c.1900: a bonne with one of the nuns
Courtesy of: Amiens, Société des Antiquaires de Picardie (en dépôt aux Arch.
dép. de la Somme) 14FI 15/24*

The building to which little Yvonne was taken in 1905 was constructed around 1860, replacing outdated facilities on rue de Beauvais with a modern, light and airy hospice. Still standing today, from the outside it has changed little since it was built. The large stone and red brick building spans four floors. The frontage stretches 50 metres along the boulevard and ranks of large windows frame the wide stone entrance in the centre. The windows were placed high, preventing anyone inside from looking out or outside from looking in. The name Hospice Saint-Charles is carved into the decorative arched stone outlining the roof above the entrance. The words '*Maison de Retraite*' appear above the name, added in a later era when the hospice was used as a retirement home. Nowadays, it houses the library of the University of Picardie Jules Verne.

To a young child, the hospice looked enormous and forbidding. Once inside, Yvonne was brought to the admissions office where nuns greeted her. Unless they were very kind and gentle, the sight alone of their habits and dramatic headwear, shaped like the full sails of a galleon

7: A MOTHER'S DESPERATION

ship, might induce trembling lips in a little girl of three and a half. Just being in this huge, alien place after Victorine's tiny cottage was daunting enough without the attention of strange adults. Yvonne longed for Victorine's comforting presence, not understanding she would never see her '*Maman*' again. A doctor examined her, possibly for the first time in her life, before she was registered and taken to the girl's dormitory.

It was winter and the cavernous rooms of the hospice were chilly and draughty. As usual, the hospice was understaffed and overcrowded with vulnerable souls of all ages. After a simple supper, eaten in silence at a refectory table with the other children, one of the older girls put Yvonne to bed as night fell. There was no one to comfort her. She fell asleep quickly, exhausted from the journey and the strangeness of the day. None of the girls in the dormitory with Yvonne that night had been there long. The hospice was merely a temporary holding pen and clearing house for abandoned and orphaned children, while foster homes were found for them.

Abandoned or orphaned girls, Hospice Saint-Charles c.1900 Courtesy of: Amiens, Société des Antiquaires de Picardie (en dépôt aux Arch. dép. de la Somme) 14FI 15/25

Another photo in the archive collection shows a small group of girls with some of the hospice staff. They are clustered around a small piano, and in the background are what appear to be a crib and beds, neatly made with fresh white covers. The photo is carefully composed and the children face the camera with varied expressions. Some look uncertain, serious, while others are half-smiling and look more confident. All appear to be well-fed, clean and presentable. The staff members look like well-meaning, no-nonsense individuals, although a dark-haired woman towards the back on the right wears a rather stern expression. The photo implies a good staff-to-child ratio; however, this was not the case. Older girls admitted to the hospice were expected to work to supplement the labour available, in particular helping with younger children. On the front row of the photo there is a little girl in a white smock dress and a bow in her long dark hair who looks roughly the same age as Yvonne was on her arrival. Maybe it is Yvonne herself.

It was traumatic for all children taken from a familiar home, and the people they knew, to the hospice. Yvonne was no exception. Physically, the children were cared for well, with nutritious food and medical care provided. But there was little emotional support and an absence of reassuring hugs to calm a disorientated, tearful child when they first arrived. Yvonne did not stay at the hospice long on this occasion. However, she would find herself in a hospice again many times over the next sixteen years.

Part Three: The Allery Years, February 1905 – June 1916

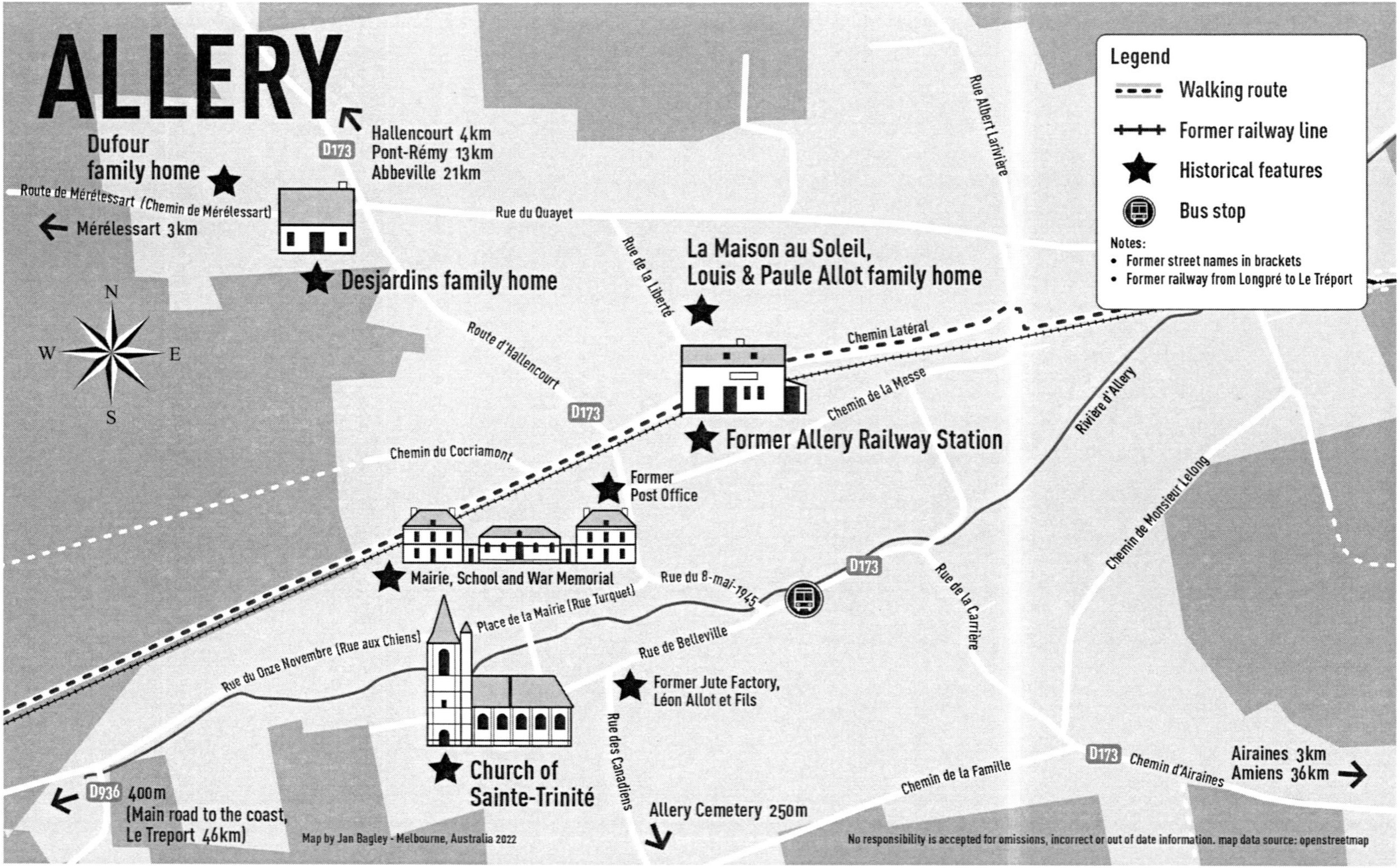

ALLERY
Hallencourt 4km
Pont-Rémy 13km
Abbeville 21km
D173
Dufour family home
Route de Mérélessart (Chemin de Mérélessart)
Mérélessart 3km
Rue du Quayet
Rue Albert Larivière
Legend
Walking route
Former railway line
Historical features
Bus stop
Notes:
• Former street names in brackets
• Former railway from Longpré to Le Tréport
Desjardins family home
Rue de la Liberté
La Maison au Soleil, Louis & Paule Allot family home
N
W
E
S
Route d'Hallencourt
Chemin Latéral
Chemin de la Messe
Former Allery Railway Station
Rivière d'Allery
Chemin du Cocriamont
Former Post Office
Chemin de Monsieur Lelong
Mairie, School and War Memorial
Rue du 8-mai-1945
Rue de la Carrière
Place de la Mairie (Rue Turquet)
Rue du Onze Novembre (Rue aux Chiens)
Rue de Belleville
Former Jute Factory, Léon Allot et Fils
Rue des Canadiens
Church of Sainte-Trinité
Chemin de la Famille
Chemin d'Airaines
Airaines 3km
Amiens 36km
D936 400m
(Main road to the coast, Le Treport 46km)
Allery Cemetery 250m
Map by Jan Bagley - Melbourne, Australia 2022
No responsibility is accepted for omissions, incorrect or out of date information. map data source: openstreetmap

8: A Place to Call Home

THE FRENCH STATE care system for orphaned and abandoned children was based on fostering. Partly this was because foster care was cheaper than placing children in orphanages, but the state also believed it was better for a child to be raised in a family environment.

Some orphanages did exist, run by religious orders outside of state control, accepting children between the ages of five and thirteen. Conditions were extremely harsh, with children put to work for twelve hours a day. The girls sewed garments and even the youngest was expected to learn very quickly to make buttonholes to an acceptable standard. It was an incredibly difficult childhood, devoid of love and nurture, which destined girls either for a life in domestic service or in the religious order themselves.

Providing kind foster parents were found for Yvonne, it was better for her to be in state care than in an orphanage. She remained at Hospice Saint-Charles just a few days while arrangements were made. Normally, the first step when a child was abandoned was to search for the mother, which could take weeks. The brevity of Yvonne's stay suggests every effort to trace Marie had already been exhausted.

Satisfied that Marie would not be found, the state acted decisively. It severed the ties between Marie and Yvonne completely and utterly, making it almost impossible for them ever to reunite. At most, Marie would have the right to know if her daughter was still alive, nothing more. For her part, Yvonne had to wait until she turned twenty-one even to be told her mother's name.

Until the end of the 19th century, society tended to blame the poor for their own misfortune. There was little sympathy for their plight. Thankfully, opinion had begun to shift by the start of the 20th century. Poor single mothers and their offspring were increasingly seen as victims who deserved help. But it was still generally assumed that if a mother abandoned her child she was fundamentally incapable of parenting, and the state should take over the role.

Hence the state became Yvonne's parent, or more specifically the department of the Somme, through the office of Assistance Publique. It would protect and educate her, with the goal of moulding her into a good, law-abiding, hard-working citizen. Achieving this was a matter of national pride. In return, Yvonne was expected to obey the adults in her life and conform to what was required of her. Yvonne had joined the ranks of France's *enfants de l'Assistance*. She was just one child among tens of thousands of children in state care in early 20th-century France.

❖ ❖ ❖ ❖ ❖

On Monday 6 February 1905, during a bitterly cold spell in northern France, little Yvonne left the hospice and was taken back to the station at Amiens. She was again accompanied by an adult who didn't know her, a social worker or possibly a nun. This time she was taken onto a train bound for Abbeville, changing trains there for the branch line to the village of Allery. Shivering with cold and bewilderment, Yvonne was led on foot from Allery station to chemin de Mérélessart where her foster mother was waiting to welcome her. Assistance Publique always dealt with the foster mother, not the father. Although two-parent families were deliberately chosen, men weren't regarded as having a role in child-rearing, especially when it came to girls. The foster mother's name was Valentine Desjardins.

Abbeville station as it looked when Yvonne arrived there in 1905

8: A PLACE TO CALL HOME

Valentine Desjardins[8] (née Billet) was 28 years old. Her husband was 32-year-old Alfred Desjardins,[9] a chimney sweep. The couple had been married for six years[10] and had no children of their own. Fostering not only brought in much-needed additional income but provided labour in the home. At a time when daily life involved never-ending manual work, it was normal and necessary for all children, except those born to wealthy parents, to help with chores. Like all foster mothers, Valentine received bonuses for raising children long-term. The amount she earned for each foster child decreased as the child grew and was able to provide more labour.

Valentine answered the knock on her cottage door and brought little Yvonne in to warm up by the stove. The person who delivered her to Valentine stayed just long enough to complete any business. Like all foster mothers, there were instructions Valentine was expected to follow.

As the adults talked, Yvonne timidly eyed her new surroundings, which were homely and resembled the home she had left in Thiepval. She was too young to understand what was going on. Valentine did her best to ease Yvonne's confusion and distress. The Desjardins were experienced foster carers and were already fostering an older girl, Marie-Rose Douchet. Marie-Rose was 11 years old and at school on the cold Monday of Yvonne's arrival. After school, Valentine was glad of her help with settling and reassuring her new foster sister.

The Desjardins' cottage was to be Yvonne's home for the next eleven years. It became the only home she ever really knew as a child. Valentine and Alfred would provide vital stability and security throughout most of her formative years. They would give her roots, a sense of family and of belonging to a community. That she stayed with them so long suggests they were very fond of her and she was happy in their care.

Not all *enfants de l'Assistance* were as fortunate. Some foster parents took in children purely for the money they could earn and some were undoubtedly cruel. Younger children were more attractive because of the higher rate paid for them. Consequently, some *enfants de l'Assistance* were deliberately moved on by foster mothers in favour of a more profitable younger child.

---

8   Valentine Marie Rosalie Billet was born 14 April 1876 in Amiens. Her parents were Valentin Emile Octave Billet and Amélia Marie Bourgeois.

9   Alfred Desjardins was born 8 June 1872 in Amiens (according to his death certificate; his birth cannot be found in the Amiens birth records).

10 Valentine and Alfred Married in Amiens on 23 March 1899.

Allery nestles in a verdant valley although the thin river running through it is often dry, flowing only after heavy rain and eventually connecting into the River Somme. The village is in the administrative district of Abbeville, the nearest town. Valentine and Alfred lived in the Quayet neighbourhood, a short climb up from the heart of the village on the north side of the valley. Their rented cottage stood on chemin de Mérélessart, today called route du Mérélessart, a road leading out into open countryside and farmland towards the neighbouring hamlet of Mérélessart.

Chemin de Mérélessart c.1900: the Desjardins' cottage was in the far distance on the left

There is no record of their exact address, but census information shows just seven households on chemin de Mérélessart in 1906. Quayet was a quiet spot on the outskirts of the village. An older resident in Allery today, who grew up on chemin de Mérélessart, still remembers it as a close-knit community, a sort of 'village within a village'. Most residents, like Valentine and Alfred, lived in humble, single-storey cottages. Judging by the order of the census information, the Desjardins' home was the fifth counting away from the crossroads with route d'Hallencourt, on the southern side. There was also a grand villa at the far end of the street, the last house on the right at the exit to the village. Set back behind wrought iron gates and a spacious front garden, wealthier people lived here, by the name of Dufour.

An undated photo, probably taken in the early 1900s, shows the view

8: A PLACE TO CALL HOME

looking down chemin de Mérélessart from the crossroads. There are two cafés on opposite corners of the junction, a large wooden crucifix standing outside Café Travet on the left. If the cafés were still in business at the time of the 1906 census, the owners were not relying on them as their main source of income, because none of them described their profession as 'café proprietor'. Monsieur Travet of Café Travet is listed as a carpenter and perhaps the crucifix was his work. Immediately beyond the cafés, the cottages of chemin de Mérélessart can be seen on both sides of the road. One of these was Valentine and Alfred's home. The photographer included villagers in his composition and it is intriguing to think Yvonne, Valentine and Alfred might even be among them. The scene today is a completely recognisable but deserted view. The corner cafés have long since been converted to homes but the crucifix outside the former Café Travet remains.

Allery today is a community of about 800 people, including young families who have moved into the village to enjoy rural peace and quiet. Residents of working age drive 40 kilometres or more to jobs in Amiens or beyond, returning home to their dormitory commune. The village covers a fairly large area, hinting at its more vibrant past, when generations of the same family lived out their entire lives there. There is a mairie and a primary school but the last remaining shop and café/bar closed in 2022. The last train pulled out of Allery station in the mid-1970s, when the branch line closed. Now the station building stands neglected and overgrown, the name 'Allery' fading on the brickwork.

Derelict railway station buildings at Allery

The village church of Sainte-Trinité dates to the 17th century and is a protected national monument. These days the village doesn't have its own parish priest and mass is only held at Sainte-Trinité once every two or three months. Yet it was once the heart of the community. Around 1900, a few years before Yvonne arrived, some rare statues dating to the 16th century were rediscovered in the church. They had been hidden from view for centuries and the find caused quite a stir of excitement locally. The bells of Sainte-Trinité still strike the hour, a reverberation from Yvonne's childhood.

Then, Allery was a thriving, self-contained community where people could live, work, shop and socialise without ever leaving the village. It was home to more than 1,000 people who spoke a local Picardie language, unique to the Abbeville area. French was the official language, and Picard was not allowed in school for example. Photos from the late 19th and early 20th century give a fascinating glimpse of daily life. Outside the post office, grocery stores and cafés, people go about their business and children play in the street. The railway station, connecting Allery to Abbeville, and even linking to Paris, is a hive of activity. It was the kind of place where everyone knew everyone else.

Street scene, Allery, early 20th century. Rue Turquet is today called place de la Mairie

Allery was a centre for jute cloth weaving, with eight factories in its heyday, each owned by a local family. By 1910, the industry was adapting to change and beginning to mechanise. One of the factories – Dufour Frères – was owned by the Desjardins' neighbours, the Dufour family.

8: A PLACE TO CALL HOME

The jute industry provided much of the employment in Allery for men and women. They produced potato sacks, mattresses and hessian for the building trade. In wartime, production would turn to sandbags and cloth for camouflaging potential targets from German bombers.

Another jute business – Allot et Fils – was owned by the Allot family, who employed around 25 weavers and other staff. Léon Allot and his family lived in a house adjacent to the factory on place de la Ville (today called place Général Leclerc). The factory's tall chimney stack, which can be seen from rue des Canadiens, is all that remains today of Allery's once-booming jute industry. By the 1960s it was clear jute manufacturing in Allery had no future, the victim of overseas competition. As Léon's son Louis Allot reached retirement, the factory closed and the next generation went into the restaurant trade, opening 'Le Pont d'Hure' in 1965. The names of these once-flourishing jute cloth producers, Allot and Dufour, would prove to be significant in Yvonne's life.

Gradually, after the trauma of being wrenched from the world she knew in Thiepval, Yvonne settled into her new life with her foster family in Allery. She was too young when she left Thiepval to retain clear memories of her earliest years there and Allery was simply 'home'.

9: Growing Awareness

AS THE YEARS passed and Yvonne grew, she thrived under the protective wing of her foster parents, Valentine and Alfred Desjardins. There were plenty of other children in the Quayet neighbourhood. In the cottage next door to the Desjardins lived the Poiret family,[11] whose youngest daughter Marie was the same age as Yvonne. Two doors away lived a couple called Albert and Charlotte Mullier, similar in age to Alfred and Valentine. Albert was a builder by trade. Their daughter Jeanne was just two years older than Yvonne and later evidence suggests the two families were close, Yvonne forming a special bond with 'Madame Charlotte', as we shall see.

Yvonne, Jeanne Mullier and Marie Poiret, living next to each other on chemin de Mérélessart, were natural playmates. They joined in games with other children in the neighbourhood, including the Dufour boys, Sosthène and his little brother Pièrre, living in the grand villa opposite the Desjardins.

Allery station in the early 1900s

---

[11] Berthe Poiret was widowed by the time of the 1911 census.

9: GROWING AWARENESS

The road outside was their playground, for games of hopscotch and tag after the day's chores were done. Traffic was rare and the only sounds were the children's voices rising above gentle birdsong, a cock crowing and the bark of a neighbour's dog. In the distance, the church bells rang out the hours. The whistle and puff of steam trains, arriving and departing the station, carried on the wind. Occasionally a horse-drawn wagon would make its way down the road, the driver calling out to the children to stand clear, or an agricultural labourer would pass by, pushing before him a bale of hay on a hand cart.

Childhood was very different in early 20th-century rural France to what we know today. The labour children provided was very important to running the home and working the land. Yvonne's childhood was much like other children in Allery. Most villagers were poor. From a young age, children had chores to do before being sent outside to play. In Yvonne's case, as an *enfant de l'Assistance*, helping at home was part of the deal for the Desjardins, and with no children of their own, it was part of their motivation for fostering.

Yvonne's situation was not at all unusual. Besides Yvonne and her foster sister, there were other *enfants de l'Assistance* in the neighbourhood, including two girls, Marie and Blanche, both a few years older than Yvonne, living just around the corner. The scale of child abandonment, and the policy of foster care, meant there were *enfants de l'Assistance* in all communities. A village the size of Allery would have around fifty at any one time. By law, local mayors were permitted to accept up to five *enfants de l'Assistance* per hundred inhabitants. Some mayors, under pressure from local residents, resisted the full quota. The bourgeoisie, whose votes the mayor needed, were not always keen to have *enfants de l'Assistance* in their midst. They feared such children would turn into vagabonds, thieves and delinquents, plaguing their community with petty crime.

Sadly this was sometimes true. Unsociable, even criminal, behaviour was not an uncommon result of the emotional damage and suffering many *enfants de l'Assistance* endured. The writer Jean Genet, abandoned as a baby in Paris in 1911, is an example. He was deeply affected by his start in life, despite good foster parents. As a youth, he drifted into a life of crime. His creative talent was discovered while he was in prison, and against the odds, this eventually led him away from the path of poverty and delinquency. Others were less fortunate.

Like all *enfants de l'Assistance*, the authorities kept an eye on Yvonne through inspection visits and examinations by a doctor. The state tried to ensure all children were looked after properly, and records were kept throughout Yvonne's time in care. But their checks were infrequent, typically just once a year, unless there was a problem. The notes recording her welfare were brief and perfunctory, perhaps written in haste by overworked officials.

The social worker who carried out the first annual visit, on 11 March 1906, noted that Yvonne was strong, in good health, and that she was in a very good placement with the Desjardins. The record for May 1907, shows that she remained in good health apart from slight impetigo on her scalp, and that she was well looked after. Happily, the situation was the same in 1908 and 1909; the record for 1910 says she was in robust health, well-behaved and the placement continued to be successful.

Evidently, Yvonne was thriving in the care of the Desjardins. She was very much part of the family and the cottage on chemin de Mérélessart was her home. The couple's living standards were perhaps a small notch above those of Victorine and Adolphe in Thiepval, on account of Alfred doing more skilled work. By the time of the 1911 census, Alfred was working in some capacity with zinc, probably roofing work or repairing the flashing on chimneys. The following description of how their cottage might have looked inside is based on a typical peasant home of that time in Boulogne-sur-Mer, northern France.

Fisherman's cottage (Maison de la Beurière), Boulogne-sur-Mer, as it would have looked around 1900. The Desjardins' kitchen may have looked very similar

The front door opened into a parlour with a small black stove squatting on four ornate feet in the fireplace. A pair of flat irons and a coffee pot stood ready for use on its hot plates and a thick cloth for handling them hung over a side rail, together with a poker to stoke the fire inside. The mantlepiece was dressed with a length of lace-trimmed white cotton, on which stood a clock, a few ornaments, a small statue of the Virgin Mary and an oil lamp.

On the wall above hung a framed black and white photographic portrait of Valentine and Alfred dressed in their Sunday best. A table covered in a white, lace-trimmed cloth stood in the centre of the room, a set of wooden chairs with curved backs around it. The parlour was used mainly for special occasions and receiving visitors, including the Assistance Publique inspectors, the doctor and the landlord when he came for the rent.

There was a bedroom with a double bed for Valentine and Alfred, a washstand and a wardrobe containing their few clothes, much of it worn and patched, some spare linens and blankets. The main living space was at the back of the cottage, and it was here the two girls slept on bunks in a cosy alcove next to the kitchen area. The family spent most of its time here, gathered around a small kitchen table where they prepared food, ate, sewed, read and talked about their day. Valentine cooked all their meals on the range in the kitchen, which was larger than the parlour stove, with hot plates on top, two small ovens and a chamber for heating water fitted with a tap. On the mantlepiece above the range stood the coffee grinder, ceramic jars of salt and pepper, and a pair of oil lamps for light by which to cook. The range also heated the room and laundry was dried on a wooden stand in front of it when the weather was too wet or cold to hang it outside.

On a dresser along a side wall were a jug and pitcher for washing hands and faces. A panel fixed to the wall next to it held a mirror, a beaker for toothbrushes and a small towel. Shelving occupied another wall, on which were arranged tins of cocoa, flour, sugar, coffee beans and chicory. The latter was mixed with the coffee, which was more expensive, to eke it out. Enamel and copper pots, pans, ladles and strainers were suspended on hooks from the lowest shelf. On a nail by the back door hung a tin bathtub, used once a week before church on Sunday. The family shared the bath water. Alfred, who did grimy manual work all week, went last. The back door opened onto a small cobbled yard with an earth WC and a shelter for storing brooms, pails and Alfred's tools. His work clothes hung here too, dull with dirt. In the small garden or potager, which overlooked open countryside, Valentine and Alfred grew vegetables to feed the family throughout the year.

The girls helped around the house, assigned jobs appropriate to their age. This was also preparation for their anticipated future, a life in domestic service. Valentine began by showing her girls simple tasks such as how to grind the coffee and stir the butter into the petit pois, small skills that Yvonne would one day pass on to her young granddaughter Jan. They learnt to sweep the tiled floor of the cottage, beat dust from the rag rugs over a line in the garden, weed the potager and pick tomatoes for lunch. As they grew older, they fetched water from the pump and collected firewood in the nearby woods.

The routines of daily life were hard, predictable and certain. They were punctuated by the annual saints' days, public holidays and harvest festival, when the village came alive with colourful processions, music and dancing. These occasions were the highlights of the year. They strengthened the bonds of the Allery community and gifted Yvonne precious memories of happy and carefree times.

Sainte-Trinité Church, Allery, early 20th century

On Sundays, the Desjardins took their foster daughters to church. Assistance Publique sometimes offered financial incentives for foster parents to send children to church, but evidence suggests the Desjardins were, like most of the villagers, regular church-goers. It was natural for them to raise children in their care in the Catholic faith. This influence in her formative years was perhaps why, much later, Yvonne insisted her own children were raised in the Catholic tradition.

Perhaps very occasionally on a public holiday, in the summertime when the sun shone, the Desjardins took the girls on a trip to the seaside. The bay of the Somme, its smooth pale sands gleaming under an endless opal sky, was only a short train ride away. At Saint-Valery-sur-Somme, Yvonne

9: GROWING AWARENESS

and her foster sister could run excitedly along the promenade, past the majestic holiday villas owned by wealthy Parisians, to see who reached the beacon first. Happy seaside memories would one day be replayed by Yvonne, watching her own children play on the beach at Boulogne-sur-Mer.

Generally, it was a contented, settled existence for Yvonne. But as she grew older, she became aware Valentine and Alfred were not her real parents and Marie-Rose was not her real sister. By the time of the 1911 census, Marie-Rose had moved on and a girl called Marguerite Bardon, five years younger than Yvonne, had replaced her. It is likely Marie-Rose and Marguerite were also, like Yvonne, the abandoned daughters of single mothers working as *domestiques* in Paris. Losing the companionship of an older 'sister' and acquiring a new, younger one was unsettling, increasing Yvonne's awareness of being in foster care.

Other things made Yvonne feel different too. She knew officials from Assistance Publique did not visit children who had real parents or deliver their clothes. Once a year, she and her foster sister received a set of cotton garments for summer and woollen ones for winter. They were standard issue according to the age of the child, so although the clothes were new, they didn't necessarily fit well. The girls' attire made them stand out from other children on both counts. Yvonne also understood that one day, like Marie-Rose, she too would have to leave the Desjardins.

It was natural for Yvonne to ask Valentine questions about where she had come from and who her real mother was. Valentine almost certainly knew nothing about Yvonne's first years, and perhaps answered simply and truthfully that she had come from the hospice in Amiens. The authorities told foster parents little about a child's background, because the policy was to keep *enfants de l'Assistance* in the dark about their birth parents, to prevent attempts to trace them. Telling the foster parents would risk information being shared with the child. When a census took place in Allery, in the column for recording the place of birth of each individual in the household, no location was given for either Yvonne or her foster sisters. Instead, next to their names, it simply says '*pupille Somme*', meaning a child in the care of the Somme local authority.

The inspector visiting in 1911 reported that Yvonne was clean, in good health, and had started her education. She was ten years old. The compulsory school ages were 6 to 13 years, but Yvonne, like other *enfants de l'Assistance*, was treated differently. Foster parents often denied children part of their education because they needed them to work either in the home or in the fields. It was an accepted part of the arrangement, although the authorities did encourage foster parents to send children to school by offering extra payments to compensate for the loss of labour.

Allery school and mairie, early 20th century

Located in the centre of the village, the school adjoined the mairie and was a fifteen-minute walk down the hill from Quayet. The same 19th-century red brick buildings are still in use as the mairie and school today and from the outside are almost completely unchanged.

In the early part of the 20th century, girls and boys were taught separately. A photo of the school taken around 1905, the year Yvonne arrived in Allery and six years before she became a pupil there, shows the girls and boys lined up in ranks outside their respective entrances, about forty of each.

Yvonne entered the school yard each morning through a gateway to the left of the mairie, with the words *École de Filles* (Girls' School) inscribed in the stone lintel above the gate. There was no school uniform but like the other girls Yvonne wore a mid-length dress with a high waistband, high neck and long sleeves, with dark stockings. On her feet she wore leather boots, laced or buttoned up to finish at mid-calf. Her long dark hair was tied back from her face with a plain ribbon. The boys had their own entrance to the right of the mairie. A brick wall separated the two halves of the playground to ensure girls and boys did not mix even at play.

Inside, the girls were taught together in their school room, and the boys in theirs, all ages learning side-by-side. During lessons, the children sat in neat rows at wooden desks with ink wells, into which they dipped their pen nibs. Two teachers taught the girls and another two the boys. One of each pair of teachers was senior to the other and held the title '*Direc-*

9: GROWING AWARENESS

trice'. There was a change of *Directrice* in 1911, the year Yvonne started at the school. The new *Directrice*, Mademoiselle Amélie Ternois, was one of Yvonne's teachers.

Yvonne's school days were not always easy. Like all *enfants de l'Assistance* in class, she was behind for her age because of the delay in starting school. She was sometimes a target for spiteful comments about her parentless status from other children. However, not everyone was unkind. Outside school, besides her playmates in the Quayet neighbourhood, Yvonne formed a special friendship with a boy called Louis Allot. His family owned one of Allery's jute manufacturing businesses. He was the only son of Léon Allot and his wife Camille. According to the censuses of 1906 and 1911, they lived with Louis' widowed grandmother and owner of the business, Marie Allot. Their house on place de la Ville was adjacent to their factory, where Léon was foreman (the business eventually transferred to his name in 1917).

Born in 1902, Louis was very close in age to Yvonne. However, this friendship between a girl and a boy of quite different social standings is something of an enigma for the era. They were not, of course, taught together at school. It seems likely they met because of Louis' friendship with Yvonne's neighbour, Sosthène Dufour, who lived in the elegant villa opposite the Desjardins' cottage on chemin de Méréléssart. The Dufour family were also in the jute manufacturing trade. Somehow, the friendship formed in childhood between Louis and Yvonne, and by extension with Sosthène, lasted a lifetime. For Yvonne, it was an enduring and treasured connection to the village she called home. It is interesting that Yvonne's most enduring friendships appear to have been with boys.

Among Louis and Sosthène's circle of childhood friends was a younger girl called Marguerite Poccardi, who spent much of her childhood in Allery. Yvonne undoubtedly knew her too. Marguerite was born in 1907 to Italian parents who owned a restaurant in Paris. Poccardi's, as it was known, occupied a substantial plot on the corner of rue Favart and boulevard des Italiens in the 2nd arrondissement. Established in the 19th century, by the early 1900s it was one of the most famous restaurants in Paris. The artist Picasso is believed to have been among the clientele.

Fully occupied with running the restaurant, Marguerite's parents took their daughter to live with Louis' mother's family, the Le Blonds, in Allery.[12] We do not know what the connection was between the Poccardis

---

12 Marguerite Poccardi does not however appear in either the 1906 or 1911 census. This could be because she was absent when the census was conducted, perhaps staying in Paris with her parents.

and the Le Blonds or how the arrangement came about, but perhaps the two families were friends. Although Louis was five years older than Marguerite, it is believed they were close growing up, perhaps because neither had a sibling.

In much later years, Yvonne mentioned to her children a 'sister' called Marguerite, saying she did not get on well with her. The true identity of this 'sister' is not clear. Yvonne would sometimes make vague references to her 'father', 'sister' and even a 'brother'. No doubt she was thinking of real people, people at the heart of her life, even though they were not related to her. Possibly the 'sister' she mentioned was her younger foster sister, Marguerite Bourdon, who joined the Desjardins household when Yvonne was about ten years old. However, she may have been referring to Marguerite Poccardi, who was often at Louis' side when she spent time with him.

Marguerite Poccardi
Photo courtesy of Frédéric Defente, grandson of Louis Allot

Tragically, Marguerite Poccardi died very young. She was buried in the Père Lachaise cemetery in Paris. The contemporary American artist Carson Barnes, who specialises in creating photo-real images from statues, created a striking picture of Marguerite Poccardi in 2016. In his commentary on the

9: GROWING AWARENESS

piece, he says, 'Marguerite Poccardi died in 1920 at the age of twelve; she was a bright, good-humored, active girl, vibrantly healthy, with a bit of an outdoorsy tan, on her way to womanhood when she was cut down abruptly by the "Spanish" influenza that carried off millions. Her wealthy and loving parents wished her commemorated in marble, and had the famed sculptor Boucher immortalize her; she's buried in Paris, where I photographed her statue in 2016. To depict her is to celebrate her.'

◆ ◆ ◆ ◆ ◆

By the time social workers made their annual inspection visit in 1912, little had changed. Yvonne was still in good health and the placement was again described as good and 'clean'. As Yvonne approached her eleventh birthday, attention turned to her religious education.

Foster parents were encouraged to send children for religious instruction between the ages of ten and twelve and to receive first communion. However, the first concern was baptism, a pre-requisite for first communion. Since it was almost impossible for anyone to find out if an abandoned child had already been baptised, it had to be assumed they had not. Consequently, it was not uncommon for *enfants de l'Assistance* to be baptised at the late age of between ten and twelve.

Yvonne was no exception. She was baptised in a small, brief ceremony on Saturday 11 May 1912 at Sainte-Trinité, just a month short of her eleventh birthday. The record states she was baptised '*sous condition*', meaning it was not known whether she had already been baptised. Almost certainly she had not, and neither had her sister Henriette. Their names are absent from the baptism records for Thiepval and it is very unlikely Marie had the time or energy to arrange for their baptism before taking them out of Paris.

Yvonne's baptism record also names two godparents, Marie and Henry Guidon. The census of 1911 reveals they were a sister and brother, aged seventeen and fourteen respectively in 1912, who lived with their parents, Emile and Blanche, on Haut de Quayet, not far from the Desjardins. Perhaps the local priest, Abbé Boucher, suggested them as godparents, two responsible teenagers in his congregation, who Yvonne knew and could look up to as positive guiding influences.

Yvonne's first communion followed shortly after her baptism and two years later she was confirmed in the Catholic faith. These religious milestones were special moments in Yvonne's young life. They were rare, precious occasions when she was the centre of attention and she was celebrated.

Abbé Boucher officiated at all three ceremonies. A popular young priest with a passion for music, he had arrived in Allery in 1910. He embraced and encouraged musical talent among his parishioners. Hymns sung at Sainte-Trinité were usually accompanied by the harmonium and a now obsolete brass instrument with keys called the ophicléide. The church organ, a small, but rare and important instrument dating to 1840, was reserved for playing only on special occasions.

Abbé Boucher wrote his own musical compositions and in 1935 he recorded a 78rpm record of his original work. The singer on the recording was Madame Paule Allot, the mother of Yvonne's friend Louis, who by then was also the regular organist at Sainte-Trinité.

For thirty years, Abbé Boucher diligently served the parish. Everyone knew him and he was well-loved. He died suddenly during midnight mass at Sainte-Trinité on Christmas Eve 1940, shocking the entire community. He was greatly missed.

❖ ❖ ❖ ❖ ❖

In 1913, the year Yvonne turned twelve, the notes for the annual inspection state she was 'quite robust', would make a very good worker but had 'no aptitude for studies'. She had, however, started to sew and mend.

The record for 1914 describes Yvonne as a beautiful young girl in good health, in a good foster placement. She was about to receive her education certificate. She had passed the statutory tests and completed her formal schooling.

Yvonne had attended school for no more than four years. She left in the summer of 1914 to begin a dressmaking apprenticeship. This was not a choice for Yvonne, it was something she was expected to do and she was not too happy about it. The apprenticeship was arranged for her by Assistance Publique. Learning a skill or trade was the usual progression for an *enfant de l'Assistance* following school, to equip them for work and independence. Yvonne was on the usual path for a girl in her situation, her future looking reasonably assured. But there were serious troubles ahead, not only for Yvonne but for France and for the world.

10: War

WAR APPROACHED AT frightening speed, as the heat of summer 1914 intensified. The threat of invasion heightened to the point when on 2 August, a sweltering day in Allery, the French government issued a general mobilisation order. Two days later, on 4 August, Britain declared war on Germany. By now, German troops were already on French soil and pushing west.

Yvonne had little idea what the news meant but was caught up in the general atmosphere of nervous excitement and patriotism all around her. In every home in the village, in the cafés and shops and on the street corners, the outbreak of war and its implications were feverishly discussed.

The first British soldiers arrived in northern France a few days later. In London, it was already clear to the Government that Britain's small regular army would not be enough for the fight ahead. Lord Kitchener, the newly appointed Secretary of State for War, made a personal appeal, rousing the nation's young men to form a new volunteer army. By mid-August, a portrait of his unmistakable face, with impressive moustache, could be seen on posters plastered across every town and city in Britain. His steely eyes fixed their gaze on their target from every angle the poster was viewed, while his finger pointed directly at the viewer. The message was hard to ignore: 'YOUR COUNTRY NEEDS YOU'.

It was a highly effective campaign. Young men from all walks of life, many so young they were really only boys, responded in huge numbers. Propelled by a wave of patriotic fervour, they flocked to recruitment halls, which at first could not cope with the huge numbers arriving every day to enlist. Most boys thought it would be a great adventure and couldn't wait to fight the Germans. They eagerly signed up to any regiment that would take them, believing if they didn't join now, they would miss out. It was widely believed the war would be over by Christmas. Little did they realise they were signing up for a hell on earth that would consume them at a horrific rate. Eventually, the government had to introduce conscription (in March 1916) to replace the ever-growing tally of casualties.

Among the boys voluntarily joining up in early 1915 was seventeen-year-old Albert Harry Bagley[13] from Blackheath, Woolwich in London. He lived with his parents, brother and three sisters at 7 Couthurst Road, a modest terraced house of London brick in a quiet side road. Known in the family as 'Jock', he was apprenticed to Lloyds Underwriters as a marine clerk, a good job with prospects. In his free time, he was a keen rugby player, amateur boxer and swimmer. His physical fitness helped him pass the army medical examination easily.

Albert was one of 250,000 boys who lied about their age to join up. Legally, only boys over 18 years old could be accepted and 19 was the minimum age for deployment on armed service overseas. Few people had birth certificates in those days and officials turned a blind eye, reasoning that if a lad was strong, fit and willing, he would make a good soldier, so why quibble about his age? It was not unheard of for a recruiting officer to advise a boy who was truthful about being underage to go back outside, 'have a birthday or two', and then report to the desk again.

Albert was the oldest son of Mary and John Bagley. Although his parents weren't wealthy, they provided a good, stable home for their five children. A family group photo, undated but probably taken in early 1915, shows Mary and John seated either side of their children, two boys and three girls. Albert stands at the back on the left, wearing his army uniform, looking fresh-faced and eager, a smile playing on his lips. The rest of the family are dressed in their Sunday best. The portrait was perhaps taken during the short period of leave Albert was granted after his initial training, before being deployed for active service.

According to a story in the Bagley family, shortly before the family set off for the photography studio, Albert and his father had a huge row. John told his son in no uncertain terms his decision to join up was 'stupid' and the war would 'not be what you think'. John, a former military horseman, whose brother Richard had died of typhoid in the Boer War, was better placed than many parents to know. By early 1915, everyone knew the war would not end swiftly, as first thought.

John and Mary's uncertain smiles caught on camera mask their unspoken thought: if anything happened to Albert, this might be the last ever picture of the family together. Poignantly, Albert's hand rests on his mother's shoulder in a gesture of reassurance. Her expression is apprehensive. His father looks proud yet fearful, still tense from arguing with Albert,

---

13 Albert was born on 8 November 1897.

10: WAR

who appears relaxed, convinced he is doing his patriotic duty, his father's concerns brushed aside by youthful bravado.

The Bagley family, early 1915. Back row: Albert, Irene, John Gordon. Front row: Mary, Catherine, Alice and John Henry

Albert and his friends were among thousands who could not resist the excitement of what promised to be a great adventure. They egged each other on. The nearest recruiting office was at Holly Hedge House, the local regiment's HQ on Wat Tyler Road, where Albert and his friends could sign up. Like other parents of underage boys, with the call of duty sweeping the nation, it was extremely difficult for Mary and John to stand in his way. Later, some parents tried hard to recall their boys from active duty on the grounds they were underage. Few succeeded.

❖ ❖ ❖ ❖ ❖

Private Albert Bagley was assigned to the 20th Battalion of the London Regiment from Blackheath and Woolwich. His service number when he began his military service was 2490, but this would change to 630787 when there was a major re-numbering of all Territorial Forces men in 1917. Albert's battalion received the numbering range 630001 to 650000.

Details of the role and movements of Albert's unit still exist in the form of the battalion's War Diary, held by the National Archives. It was part of the duties of commanding officers to keep daily notes of events and information about the unit under their command. They were issued with pre-printed War Diary notebooks for this purpose. The officers' notes were written with a pencil held in a steady hand, sometimes even under bombardment, and give a fascinating glimpse into battalion life. They record both the monotonous routines behind the lines and the horror of front line action, in the same matter-of-fact tone.

Albert and his fellow new recruits received six weeks of intense basic training, in the St Albans area, Hertfordshire, to knock them into military shape. There were long route marches carrying heavy packs, lessons in rifle maintenance and three square meals a day. Then, on Monday 8 March 1915, they were given 'marching orders'.

The Battalion was under the command of Lieutenant Colonel Arthur Hubback, who like Albert, would survive the war. The men paraded at 5 am on the morning of Tuesday 9 March. The strength of the battalion was recorded as 31 officers, 1130 NCOs and men, 78 horses, 2 machine guns and 21 wagons. At 6 am, the battalion marched the five miles or so to Harpenden railway station to board trains bound for Southampton. That afternoon, the battalion set sail across the English Channel on four ships, the Viper, the Queen Alexandra, the Duchess of Argyll and the Trafford Hall. These had been requisitioned for military use, along with many other vessels. The Trafford Hall carried the horses and equipment.

Requisitioned for war service, the Duchess of Argyll helped transport the 20th Londons to France in March 1915

Escorted by the navy, troop ships were crossing to France daily from ports along the South coast of England, bringing fresh recruits for the Western Front. Albert, like all the men, wore a khaki coloured uniform and carried a kit bag and a Lee Enfield rifle.

The 20th Londons arrived in Le Havre in the early hours of Wednesday 10 March and disembarkation began at 7.30 am. They marched to a military camp in Le Havre, where the men spent their first night in France under canvas. The next day they received orders to proceed to the railway station. Here they were served hot drinks and rolls provided by two British women, Mrs Sidney Pitt and Mrs Haines who ran a coffee stall for troops waiting to board trains. Mrs Pitt and Mrs Haines were most likely Red Cross volunteers or public-spirited wealthy women who took it on themselves to support the war effort. The men were very grateful. But for the kindness of these women, they would have gone hungry between breakfast and 10.30 that night, when they arrived at their destination: Cassel, near Hazebrouck in French Flanders, not far from the Belgian border.

Albert's battalion stayed in this area for further intensive training until they were deemed ready to go into action for the first time in mid-April. Their first major battle came in May 1915 at Festubert, a day's march from Cassel. Naturally, the men were curious about what it would really be like in the front-line trenches. They were afraid and eager in equal measures. The sound of the guns could be heard thundering in the distance, becoming louder and louder as they approached the support trenches. From here they moved up the communication trenches leading into the front line. As they got closer and closer, they could be in little doubt about what to expect when they arrived.

Albert's war experience would prove to be typical of millions of young men. For four years they lived moment to moment, worrying only about staying alive and when they would next eat. Who died and who survived was down to chance. Luck stayed on Albert's side.

At some point in the war, he sustained a wound to the arm or shoulder. In that moment, the shock as the bullet struck made him yell and the blow knocked him to the ground. The pain kicked in only afterwards, perhaps as he reached the First Aid post, the adrenalin still pumping through his body. He kept as a souvenir the uniform tunic he was wearing at the time, ripped where the bullet or shrapnel had struck. Many years later Albert showed his torn tunic to his granddaughter Jan, evidence of that terrifying moment. Perhaps he parcelled up the tunic to send home, or maybe he was still wearing it when sent back to England to recuperate.

A note written by his sister Catherine, surviving among family documents, mentions Albert carried shrapnel in his heel and his hip. These injuries were perhaps sustained at other times to the shoulder wound. Both Catherine and Gordon, Albert's oldest son, believed he was wounded on three occasions during the course of the war. There is no surviving documentary evidence to confirm when he was wounded or where he was at the time. Yet this missing information could shed light on speculation in the Bagley family that Albert and Yvonne first met during the war.

Albert's service record, held by the National Archive, provides minimal information and does not mention his injuries. Most medical records of First World War servicemen were destroyed decades ago. Intriguingly, a fragment of his medical history can be found on the Forces War Records website. All that remains refers to 1915, when between 11 November and 8 December he was treated for a fibrous nodule on his right heel at the No.2 General Hospital at Le Havre. He had been on active service in France for nine months at this point and his battalion had already been engaged in two major battles. It is possible Albert's foot injury was sustained in the second of these, the Battle of Loos, near Lille, which lasted from 25 September to 8 October 1915. It was an early success for the 20th Londons.

The following is an extract from an account of the battalion's charge on Loos, written by Private C J Andrews, who fought with Albert.

> 'We were well in front at the attack on Loos. Our battalion has covered itself in glory. The casualty list is heavy of course, but bearing in mind the ground gained, the losses are relatively small. The position being captured, we had to hold it for four days against constant German counter attacks. That we succeeded despite empty stomachs and a merciless rain, not to mention the awful horrors with which we were surrounded, speaks volumes for the pluck and endurance of the battalion.
>
> 'We arrived in our front line trench at about 04.00 on the morning of the 25th and at about 05.30 the fun started with a most tremendous bombardment of our front line and the reserve lines with their heavy artillery and every inch of our trench seemed to be blown to Hades and the noise was deafening. I am sure that everybody was glad when at 06.30 the order was 'Over the top with the best of luck'. We had on gas helmets and after we had got as far as their front line mine got so stuffy and hot that I couldn't stick it any longer so I pulled it up and got out a cigarette and carried on.
>
> 'The most marvellous thing to me was that I wasn't hit. I certainly felt safer out in the open than in the trench, but with shrapnel bursting overhead and 'coal boxes' ploughing up the ground 20 or 30 yards away and machine gun bullets zipping all around, I literally had to assure myself that

I wasn't wounded by looking at my clothing to see if there were any holes or not, but I was all right. Almost an hour after we started we finally reached our objective, where... we had to hang on for four days, when we were relieved and went back to a village about ten miles away from the scene of up to date butchery.'

It seems Private Andrews' luck eventually ran out. A Private C Andrews of the 20th London Battalion is listed as having died on 7 November 1917.

❖ ❖ ❖ ❖ ❖

Throughout the war years, Albert's battalion was continually on the move across northern France and southern Belgium. During the second half of the war, Yvonne also moved address frequently within the department of the Somme. Tracing their movements, two points in time emerge when their paths might have crossed. However in 1915 their war-time meeting, if it happened, was at least a year away, possibly two. While Albert was getting his first tastes of trench warfare in Flanders, Yvonne was learning to sew in Allery.

11: Childhood Ending

FROM THE START of the war, there was an immediate impact on the civilians of the Somme. All men of fighting age were called up, including Yvonne's foster father, Alfred Desjardins. He was by now 42 years old, but the situation was so grave that men up to the age of 45 were conscripted into the army. Men in their forties were even deployed in the front line. Some were reservists who undertook military training every year and so were almost battle-ready. Others had received no training since their compulsory military service as young men.

Alfred Desjardins (standing) in uniform, 1915
Photo courtesy of his granddaughter, Maryline Desjardins

11: CHILDHOOD ENDING

A photo belonging to Alfred's granddaughter Maryline shows Alfred in his army uniform. It was taken at Saint Pol de Léon, Brittany, in 1915 (perhaps he had been sent there for training). He stands next to another soldier who is seated on a stool. Alfred looks ill at ease in uniform, suggesting he was not a reservist. He clasps his hands casually behind his back, his head tilted slightly to one side. His expression is serious, resigned, not lacking in confidence but not comfortable with the role thrust on him either. Weeks or months earlier he had bid '*au revoir*' to Valentine, Yvonne and Marguerite, not knowing when or if he would see them again. The parting shook them all.

As local men left for the front in the French sector to the South, so soldiers from across the British Empire began to arrive in the Somme region. Soldiers were billeted in Allery, and Yvonne and her friends saw them out and about in the village. From the vantage point of chemin Latéral, looking down over the tracks at Allery railway station, they could watch soldiers coming and going on the trains running back and forth to Abbeville.

A photo in the archives shows an Indian soldier in a turban with some local Allery residents, eager to have their picture taken with this exotic-looking man from a distant land. The Allot family were among those who lodged Indian soldiers under their roof.

An Indian soldier poses with Allery residents, 1914/15
Courtesy of Historial de la Grande Guerre – Péronne, Somme

The entire population became completely preoccupied with the war as the atmosphere of excitement rapidly gave way to fear and tension. Before long, news reached Allery that the first casualties from the front had arrived in Abbeville, a convoy of 200 wounded men on 21 August 1914, and 400 more on the 24th. They were taken to hastily created hospitals in requisitioned buildings across town. This was the beginning of a torrent of casualties into Abbeville that was to last more than four years.

Children were not sheltered from the reality of the situation. On the contrary, in such desperate times, the authorities actively mobilised children to play their part too. Patriotic duty was promoted to the fore in every aspect of a child's life at school, at home and even in the games they played. Children learnt it was right and proper to hate the enemy and to defend the nation at all costs. The French defeat in the Franco-Prussian War of 1870-71 was, after all, within living memory, and now the very existence of France was at stake.

Children were constantly reminded of the sacrifice their elders were making and were organised to help the war effort in practical ways. Dubbed *'petits poilus'* – meaning 'little soldiers' – children collected materials that could be used in the armament factories and knitted warm socks and scarves for the soldiers. Older children were put to work in the fields and factories, the labour essential to keep production going while the men were away fighting. Girls of Yvonne's age joined other villagers to help bring in the harvest or put their sewing skills to use in some way.

In late May 1915, the next entry on her file, Yvonne was almost a year into her dressmaking apprenticeship. It was not going well. Her instructor complained of her 'difficult character'. This was perhaps nothing more than typical teenage behaviour, however hormonal changes were no doubt exacerbated by what was happening in her life. Approaching her fourteenth birthday, Yvonne knew she must soon move on from her foster home and the kind, stable protection provided there. Her settled existence was coming to an end, her future full of uncertainty and fear, compounded by the war. She missed Alfred. With Alfred away fighting, Valentine cared for her foster daughters alone. All of them worried whether he would ever return.

Most children in France at that time were expected to be almost completely independent by the age of fourteen, although they were not considered to be adults until either they married or turned twenty-one. Many young girls left home to go into service at fourteen through economic necessity. But for an *enfant de l'Assistance* it was different. The

11: CHILDHOOD ENDING

home they left was not one they could return to and the support their foster mother had given was, officially at least, at an end.

For Yvonne, the thought of leaving the only home she had ever known was daunting, the tense atmosphere of the war adding to her anxiety about what would become of her. It was hardly surprising if the fear she felt inside, combined with incipient womanhood, manifested in moodiness and unwillingness to co-operate with her dressmaking instructor. It was a lot for any teenage girl to cope with. Fortunately, perhaps at Valentine's insistence or because of the war, the authorities agreed Yvonne could stay with Valentine for another year.

Just 110 kilometres away from Allery, Private Albert Bagley had very different concerns on his mind. In late May 1915, two months after landing in France, his battalion was in action at Festubert, to the east of Bethune, in the Pas-de-Calais region. The Germans shelled and shot at them in the glorious spring weather. Albert stood shoulder to shoulder with the other men, furiously fighting back. He was not yet 18 years old. Death was quickly becoming a way of life. In the lulls between the deafening fire, on either side of No Man's Land, the young soldiers, stunned and weary, cleared away the corpses of their fallen comrades. It was already feeling like a long war.

Part Four: Leaving Home,
June 1916 – June 1922

12: A Painful Parting

A YEAR LATER, on Thursday 15 June 1916, four days after her 15th birthday, and almost two years into the war, Yvonne's settled life in Allery ended. Until she reached the age of twenty-one and her majority, she would remain in the parental care of the state but in a different type of arrangement. The moment had arrived when she must start working to keep a roof over her head. It was the beginning of a progressively unsettled, difficult and unhappy period in Yvonne's life.

Assistance Publique would from now on ensure Yvonne worked to offset the cost of her care until she came of age and was no longer their responsibility. Officials found placements for her although she may have found some of the later positions herself, which was quite common among older *enfants de l'Assistance*. She was sent to households where in return for labour she received board and lodgings. It was basically a reciprocal arrangement; however, if her work and her conduct were deemed up to scratch, she also received a small wage.

Yvonne was mostly in domestic service during her remaining time in care, although there is evidence to suggest she may have used her sewing skills in some placements and undertook shop work in others. *Enfants de l'Assistance* had few occupations open to them at this time. Girls mainly worked as *bonnes*, although some had positions as seamstresses. A tiny minority worked in shops.

To begin with, Yvonne was heading for a life as a *domestique*, just like her mother before her, although at the time she knew nothing about Marie. It would be wisest to resign herself to the role and behave in the way expected of a *bonne*: polite, submissive and willing at all times. As she would soon learn, any grumbles, answering back or overstepping the mark would have consequences. It was best for her to contain the attitude that caused her dressmaking instructor to complain. She would find this more and more difficult as time went on.

Her employers would have little interest in Yvonne, the person, the motherless young girl whose start in life had been so difficult. For them, she was just a worker, the girl who does the chores. When conversation

12: A PAINFUL PARTING

among their bourgeoise friends inevitably turned to comparing the shortcomings of their *bonnes*, Yvonne was referred to only as '*ma fille*' ('my girl'). Accepting her lot would prove to be a tall order.

All young people in domestic service were vulnerable to exploitation by unscrupulous employers. An *enfant de l'Assistance* was however even more at risk, as it was known they had no family to challenge how they were treated. Assistance Publique provided only limited protection against the worst exploitation through their programme of regular inspections, but these were too infrequent to be effective. There was no effective legal protection either. The law had slowly begun to introduce rights for servants by this time, but the isolated nature of the work hid abuses from view and in reality, a *domestique* was powerless to take action.

Assistance Publique put aside part of the wages earned by young people in their care for their future. They opened a savings account for Yvonne with the Amiens branch of Caisse d'Épargne. Now one of the leading banks in France, Caisse d'Épargne was founded by philanthropists in the early 19th century to encourage the lower strata of society to save. The regular savings going onto Yvonne's account would provide a dowry for her when she turned twenty-one and left care, or got married before then. Although not obliged to do so, some foster parents set aside the 50 Franc bonus they received for keeping a child until her twelfth birthday as a dowry. This was a sign of real affection, and maybe the Desjardins did this for Yvonne.

It was an emotional scene the June morning in 1916 when Yvonne said goodbye to Valentine and her ten-year-old foster sister Marguerite. She was leaving behind the people she called family, the place she called home and all her friends. Childhood, for Yvonne, was over. She cut a poignant figure as she set off down the road, a short girl with long dark hair carrying a small bag containing few possessions. She walked with a heavy heart towards a new and uncertain life alone.

At Allery station she boarded the early morning civilian train, clutching in her hand the special permit she needed to travel under wartime regulations. Yvonne's destination was Abbeville. She had visited the town from time to time growing up, but seldom, if at all, in the previous two years because of the restrictions of war. She was full of trepidation as the train pulled away from the platform, but also curious to see for herself what was happening in Abbeville, because all kinds of tales had reached her.

In 1916 Abbeville was an important garrison and military hospital base, and had been since the start of the war. Around 40 kilometres behind the front, the town fed by rail, road and river the larger strategic base at

Amiens. The port of Abbeville, on the River Somme, was a vital link to the north coast of France and the English Channel.

Arriving at Abbeville station, Yvonne was greeted by a frenetic, noisy scene. Soldiers packed into trains bound for the front, the steam engines departing with shrill, shrieking whistles and determined chugs. Women waited anxiously to meet Abbevillois men coming home on leave while others tearfully waved farewell to their loved ones, fearful they would never see them again. News from the French sector had been dismal for months. At Verdun, 300 kilometres south-east of Abbeville, a devastating battle had been raging in the most appalling conditions since February with enormous losses. It would continue for the rest of the year.

British army lorries parked in the centre of Abbeville, 1914-18
Photo courtesy of Archives départmentales de la Somme (France), cote du document 14J77/54

Making her way on foot through the crowds, Yvonne gingerly crossed roads clogged with military traffic, mechanical and horse-drawn. She saw ranks of army lorries parked up in the town's squares and at the roadside. Cavalrymen on horseback pressed purposefully through the throng. Soldiers, mostly British but also from across the Empire, marched towards the station. In the other direction came convoys of motor-ambulances, the Red Cross displayed vividly on their khaki sides.

Cafés heaved with customers, many in uniform, spilling out onto pavement terraces. Waiters weaved deftly between the tables, dispensing coffee and collecting cash. Women chatted as they queued outside shops for the day's provisions. Wagons clattered along the cobbled streets. The low drone of a war plane passing high above added to the din. The assault to Yvonne's senses distracted her from the nerves she felt about what lay ahead.

12: A PAINFUL PARTING

Hospice Général George Dumont, rue Dumont, Abbeville
Photo courtesy of the Filles de la Charité de Saint Vincent de Paul

Yvonne's destination was Abbeville's Hospice Général George Dumont on rue Dumont, a quiet side road not far from the town centre. The building still stands, today a retirement home, and an information board at the gate explains the history. The hospice gave shelter to those in need, including abandoned children, for over two hundred years until it closed in 1976. It was run by the same religious order in charge at the hospice in Amiens, the *Filles de la Charité de Saint Vincent de Paul*. A local doctor, George Dumont, bequeathed funds to develop the current building on the site in 1873. The hospice and the road on which it stands were named in his honour.

Few records of the hospice remain from the early 20th century, partly due to the disruption and destruction of two world wars. Among surviving information is a small feature about the hospice that appeared in the local paper in 1953. At that time the hospice was caring for 250 pensioners, 70 invalids and around 20 *enfants de l'Assistance*. We do not know how many *enfants de l'Assistance* were typically at the hospice at any one time in 1916, but it seems likely the numbers were greater because of the scale of need.

Outwardly, the building has altered little since Yvonne first arrived there. At the front, the massive stone and brick building has three wings framing uniform rectangles of lawn, with iron railings on the fourth side edging the street.

The entrance was through the huge stone gateway, hung with iron gates. Yvonne lifted the latch, making the hinges squeal as she pushed a gate open and stepped inside. A vague and disturbing memory stirred, which she couldn't place, of her arrival at the hospice in Amiens as a three-year-old. She crossed the empty courtyard towards the main entrance, beneath a tall bell tower pointing like a finger towards the sky. It felt as though eyes were watching her from the ordered ranks of windows to the front and on either side of her.

Over the years ahead, Yvonne would grow used to entering the hospice and knew exactly what to expect, because she returned a number of times between work placements. But this first time, in June 1916, was nerve-wracking. In addition to its usual inhabitants, the hospice was being used to accommodate wounded soldiers and typhoid victims. It was severely overcrowded, uncomfortable, noisy and unsettling for Yvonne after the calm, familiar order of the Desjardins' cottage.

Like the hospice in Amiens, the nuns were assisted by civilian staff. The over-stretched personnel welcomed the arrival of an extra pair of hands. Once they had registered Yvonne she was immediately put to work, undertaking domestic duties and helping with the babies and younger children.

One of the nuns Yvonne encountered was the kindly 44-year-old Sister Jeanne. Renowned for her tireless hard work, approachability and ready smile, she had entered service at the hospice in 1898 and devoted the rest of her life to helping those who passed through its doors. She died in 1967 at the age of 95, continuing her work at the hospice until a few weeks before her death.

❖ ❖ ❖ ❖ ❖

Yvonne spent two days at the hospice before she was sent to her first placement, in Abbeville. This was at the home of a man called Louis Dallon. The records reveal little more than his name. He lived slightly out of town, to the south-east, in the neighbourhood of Faubourg Saint-Gilles. There is no exact address on Yvonne's file and no trace of Louis Dallon in either the 1911 or 1921 census. A business directory for 1916, the *Almanach d'Abbeville*, lists a number of people with the name Dallon resident in Faubourg Saint-Gilles. Several of them were gardeners by profession and possibly related to Louis Dallon. But Louis himself is not listed. It is impossible to know anything about him or who comprised the household Yvonne served.

If there were no other *domestiques* or female family members living there, Yvonne was expected to deal with all the cleaning, cooking, laundry and mending. She soon understood the meaning of hard work. Her days were exhausting, the work time-consuming and boring. All day long she

12: A PAINFUL PARTING

swept, dusted, polished, peeled, chopped, cooked, washed, fetched and carried, all the while listening out for the call *'viens, ma fille'* ('come here, girl').

The tools she used were big and heavy: wooden wash boards, mangles, flat irons, copper pans, scrubbing brushes, mops, pails, bellows and carpet beaters. By the end of the day, her muscles ached and she was grubby from dust and sweat, her hands sore from repeated immersion in soapy water.

Her working hours, though long, were not as crushing as her mother's had been. By this time, the first laws had been passed limiting the number of days a week and hours a day a *domestique* could be made to work. Assistance Publique no doubt attempted to enforce these for children in their care. Even if her employers did adhere to the regulations, Yvonne did not finish work until the evening and rose early from her bed the next morning to tie on her apron, roll up her sleeves and do it all again. It was a hard, lonely existence for a young girl in any circumstances and even more difficult in the midst of the war.

Yvonne also ran errands and shopped for groceries in town and headed there whenever she had some time off. She relished any chance to go out. Abbeville in 1916 was a very exciting, and sometimes dangerous, place for a teenage girl. A unique account of life in the town during the war was written by a local clergyman, Canon Le Sueur.[14] He recorded in vivid detail what it was like and the descriptions given here draw on his account.

By the time Yvonne arrived at the home of Louis Dallon, almost two years after the war began, the Abbevillois had grown accustomed to living among the cogs of an extraordinary war machine superimposed on their ordinarily quiet French town. Their familiar, pre-war rhythm of life had been completely disrupted. The British began to establish a military base at Abbeville from October 1914 and it became the headquarters of the Commonwealth lines of communication. The population rapidly swelled as troops, support staff and medical personnel flooded in. Thousands of British Empire servicemen were billeted with local residents in the town and surrounding villages. If soldiers were lodged in Monsieur Dallon's house, this added to Yvonne's daily workload.

The Abbevillois were amazed to see the diversity of soldiers arriving from all corners of the British Empire to join the fight. Most had never seen a black or Asian face before, an Indian in his turban or a Scotsman

---

[14] Canon ('Chanoine') Le Sueur kept meticulous notes throughout the war. His book 'Abbeville Pendant La Guerre 1914-18' was published in 1927.

with his curious bagpipes. By the end of 1916, thousands of Chinese workers also began to arrive, employed by the British and French governments, mainly to help build up rail capacity for military use. Abbeville became a 'kaleidoscope that reflected the colours and attitudes of all the people of the world'.[15]

A plan drawn by Canon Le Sueur identified 96 different military establishments across the town. There was everything imaginable an army needed including ammunition and map stores, laundries, a printing press, army post office, tent repair factory, officers' clubs, drivers' stations, prisoner of war camps, an anti-gas school, nurses' homes and military chapels. Two veterinary hospitals each accommodated 1,500 war horses and mules, who recuperated in huge open-air paddocks, their injuries and suffering plain for all to see. Everything possible was done to help the poor creatures recover, less from compassion but more so they could be returned to service again at the front.

Over the course of the war, several military hospitals were established in Abbeville. Some were in requisitioned buildings and mainly received French casualties. On the outskirts of town, huge tented hospital complexes were erected for wounded soldiers of the British Empire. Within three months of the start of the war, the No.2 Stationary British Hospital was created on a triangle of land leased by the British government along the route de Doullons, on the eastern edge of town. A hospital for Canadian casualties and another for South African casualties were erected alongside. The evidence on these hospitals is not entirely clear, but it seems the Canadian hospital was moved at some point, the 3rd Australian General Hospital taking its place in June 1917. The hospitals continually expanded their capacity, eventually containing enough beds for up to 1,500 patients. Even then, at times, they were completely overwhelmed with casualties.

Although at first each nation's hospital received primarily their own casualties, evidence suggests this changed over time. Each hospital began to specialise in different types of injury, accepting patients according to their medical needs rather than nationality. For example, the South African hospital specialised in fractures.

Hospitals were formed from temporary structures – wooden huts and marquees – arranged in orderly rows, the grass between them neatly mown. Everything was managed meticulously. The medical facilities

---

15 'Abbeville est le kaléidoscope qui reflèt les couleurs est les attitudes de tous les peuples de la terre' – Chanoine Le Sueur

12: A PAINFUL PARTING

and standards of hygiene were state-of-the-art, with hot running water in copper pipes, a modern convenience as yet unknown to the Abbevillois. Every possible comfort was provided for patients; however, the wards were very cold in winter. In the town centre there was also an Annexe to the No.2 Stationary Hospital, housed in a requisitioned private mansion, L'hôtel Madame Saint-Pol, at number 5 rue des Capucins.

Abbeville's peace-time population of 25,000 doubled to 50,000 during the war, placing tremendous pressure on the town's facilities and infrastructure. The strain was felt acutely by the local council, which worked with the military to accommodate tens of thousands of personnel and facilitate the extensive war operation. At the same time, the authorities had to maintain services to the civilian population and fulfil their responsibilities to the most vulnerable citizens, including *enfants de l'Assistance*, Yvonne among them.

Despite the turmoil, social workers continued to visit Yvonne regularly to check on her welfare. The variety of different handwriting in Yvonne's file shows there was no continuity and she was visited by different social workers on each occasion. No one from Assistance Publique really got to know Yvonne. After the protection of her foster family, she felt the absence of a constant adult in her life acutely.

❖ ❖ ❖ ❖ ❖

It took around twenty minutes for Yvonne to reach the town centre from Faubourg Saint-Gilles, the neighbourhood where she lived. She walked north along the wide, cobbled rue Saint-Gilles, passing on her right the pale-stone church, dating to the 15th century, that gave the district its name. It still stands today. When she reached the northern end of rue Saint-Gilles, she could pause to look in the dress shop windows, in the shade of the canopies pulled out to protect the goods displayed from sunlight. Yvonne was now in the heart of town.

All around her she witnessed the bustle and clatter of the crowded streets, the military comings and goings intermingled with ordinary shoppers and civilians going about their daily business. As always, there was feverish activity at the railway station. Hugely important for delivering soldiers, munitions and supplies to the front, it ran at full capacity day and night.

Civilian travel was severely restricted, with maybe just a couple of non-military trains running daily, one in the early morning and one in the evening. The war had precedence over the tracks, rolling stock and precious supplies of coal. This meant it was very difficult for Yvonne to visit Valentine, in Allery, when she had an afternoon off. She missed her dreadfully. She was unable to get to church at Sainte-Trinité on Sundays, breaking a habit formed during her childhood years in Allery, and depriving her of the friendship and support she knew there. Perhaps instead she ventured alone into Saint-Gilles church looking for solace and familiarity in the rituals of the Catholic faith.

A pre-war view of rue Saint-Gilles, Abbeville

Slowly she made acquaintances and a few friends in Abbeville. She got to know young women working behind the counter in the grocery store and chatted with other *bonnes* in the queue at the boulangerie. These girls had little freedom but two *bonnes*, who found themselves running errands at the same time each week, could easily arrange to rendezvous for a few minutes the following week, even if only to queue together for bread. It was a brief moment of companionship for Yvonne to walk across town with a newfound friend. As the two girls pushed through the crowds with their wicker shopping baskets over their arms, the sights and sounds of the melée around them would catch their attention. What they witnessed made them nudge one another, whisper and point, giggle and gasp.

Outside the town's many restaurants and cafés, which were packed with military personnel, they saw signs written in English which they didn't

12: A PAINFUL PARTING

understand but read 'Dining rooms for soldiers' or 'Fried potatoes a speciality'. Proprietors had been quick to adapt to their new English-speaking customers and, knowing they had plenty of money in their pocket, hiked their prices outrageously.

Attractive young French girls would catch the eye of soldiers seated on the café terraces as they passed by. Shy at first, Yvonne perhaps partially enjoyed their attention, lonely and starved of affection as she was.

Concert given by the British Army in place Saint-Pièrre (today called place Clémenceau), Abbeville 1914-18
Photo courtesy of Archives départmentales de la Somme (France), cote du document 14J85/7

Entertainment was big business in the town, because the army knew how important it was to maintain troop morale. Soldiers needed distraction in their downtime and Abbeville's three theatres and cinema were fully operational, packed every night with service personnel and civilians. The army was also mindful of the impact on civilians of their presence and looked for ways to maintain good relations. On at least one occasion the army held a public concert in place Saint-Pierre. A photo of the event survives in the town archives. Perhaps Yvonne is there, among the large crowd gathered round to hear the brass band play.

On Saturday nights and Sunday afternoons, when Yvonne had time off, she could occasionally afford to see a show with a friend. The largest and most popular cinema in Abbeville was set up by the British on boulevard

Vauban. The price of a seat was 50 centimes. It was still the era of silent movies. Film production in Europe ground to a halt during the war and it was the latest movies from Hollywood on the bill. Charlie Chaplin, Douglas Fairbanks and other big stars transported audiences far away from the dismal reality of wartime France to a magical, glittering world.

For girls, the prospect of meeting soldiers in the foyer was an added draw but they were often surprised to find the men subdued. In those dark days, the atmosphere inside auditoriums was not light-hearted, no matter how jolly the show. Yet the men craved any form of entertainment for the psychological boost it gave them. Even in the front line, soldiers with musical and comedic talent would put on improvised shows. These typically featured very dark humour, the ensuing laughter a vital pressure valve which helped the men cope.

Although there was plenty of entertainment, none of the usual peacetime celebrations went ahead. The annual calendar of saints' festivals and feast days was cancelled, even the most important national holiday, Bastille Day, on 14 July. Any weddings were brief and simple, with just the statutory four witnesses present. There were no pâtisseries or gâteaux available, only bread.

All local Frenchmen who were fit and able were away fighting, either to the south along the French sector of the Western Front or overseas. They left behind many anxious wives, daughters, mothers and sisters. These same women extended a warm welcome to the British servicemen who supplanted their husbands, fathers, sons and brothers in the towns and villages. Some women threw themselves at the foreign men in their midst. There were letters of complaint in the local paper about the shocking immorality in Abbeville and the pornography openly on display in bars and cafés. Prostitutes travelled in from Paris for the easy money to be made from British soldiers, who paid well.

Yvonne would hear talk about what was going on and saw evidence of it for herself as she went about the town. Raised with Catholic propriety by the Desjardins, she was both shocked and wide-eyed with teenage curiosity, her innocence dissolving. The atmosphere in the town was in some ways like a carnival. But the Red Cross flags on certain buildings across the town, with ambulances waiting silently outside, signalled there was no party going on.

The huge gaps men left in the local workforce were harder to fill than the empty bedrooms they left behind, which were taken immediately. Out of necessity, the authorities called on women to take up the jobs vacated

12: A PAINFUL PARTING

by the men. They stepped up admirably and, in doing so, took a significant stride forward on the long march towards gender equality.

As the war progressed, the Abbevillois became increasingly worn down by the labour shortages, rising prices, scarcity of fuel, fear of bombardment and general uncertainty. Despite this, they generally remained calm. The worst was still to come.

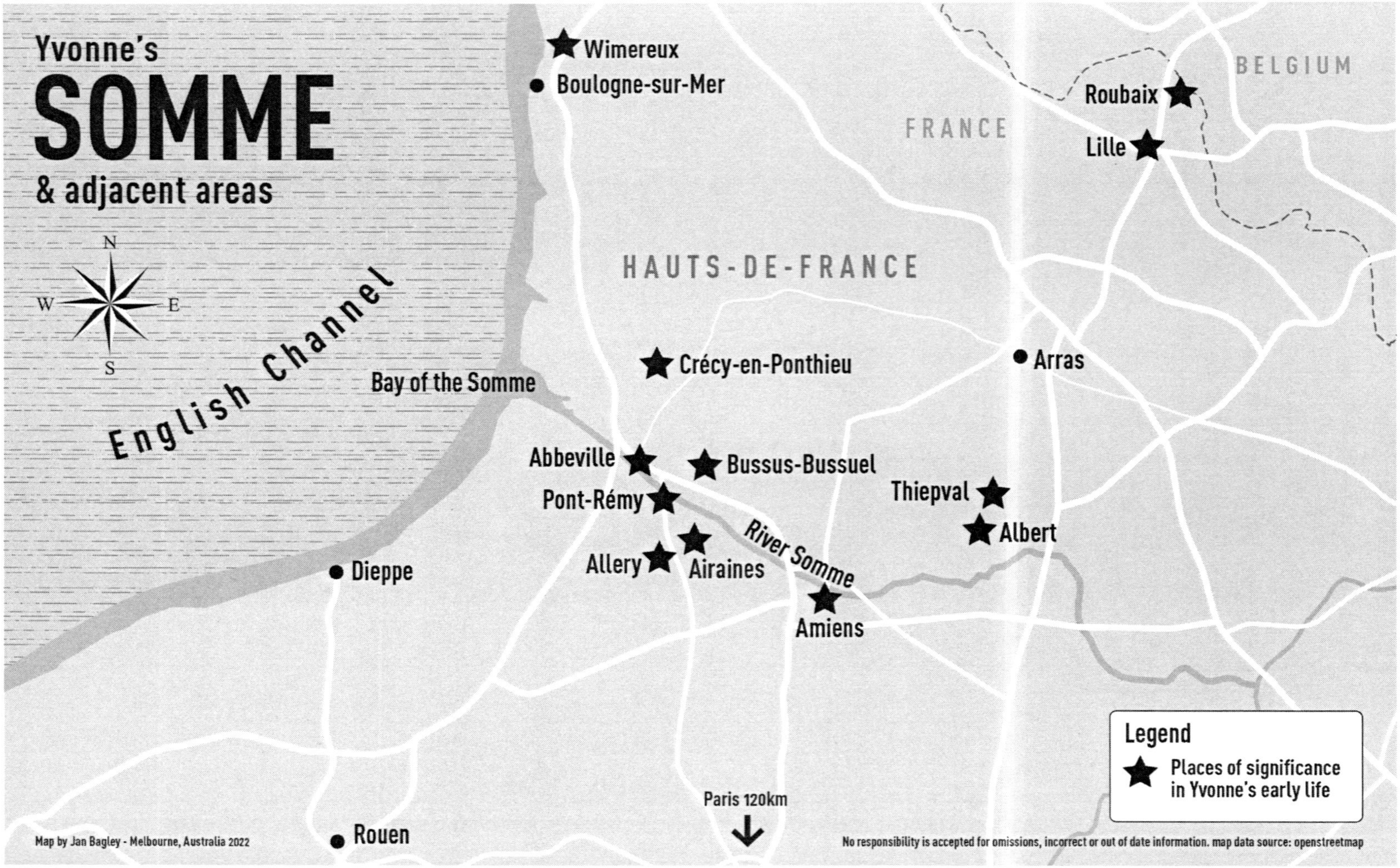

Yvonne's
SOMME
& adjacent areas
N
W
E
S
English Channel
Wimereux
Boulogne-sur-Mer
FRANCE
BELGIUM
Roubaix
Lille
HAUTS-DE-FRANCE
Arras
Crécy-en-Ponthieu
Bay of the Somme
Abbeville
Bussus-Bussuel
Pont-Rémy
Thiepval
Albert
River Somme
Allery
Airaines
Dieppe
Amiens
Legend
Places of significance in Yvonne's early life
Paris 120km
Rouen
Map by Jan Bagley - Melbourne, Australia 2022
No responsibility is accepted for omissions, incorrect or out of date information. map data source: openstreetmap

13: The Shattering of Tranquillity

THE NAME 'SOMME' comes from the Celtic word meaning 'tranquillity', a word befitting the natural peacefulness and beauty of the region's gentle green landscape. How ironic and tragic, therefore, that after the events of summer 1916, the Somme became synonymous with the carnage of war.

At 7.30 am on Saturday 1 July 1916, a clear sunny morning, just two weeks after Yvonne started her first placement in Faubourg Saint-Gilles, the British launched a major offensive: the Battle of the Somme. The attack happened along a 30 kilometres stretch of the front just east of Albert, from a point north of Thiepval towards the town of Roye to the south, crossing the River Somme at a place called Frise. Blood shed there trickled in the river for 70 kilometres before it flowed through Abbeville and onwards to the sea. The first day of the battle still holds the record as the bloodiest day in British military history, with losses on an unprecedented scale. On the first day alone there were nearly 58,000 casualties, including 20,000 dead.

Wounded soldiers began arriving at Abbeville's military hospitals by Saturday evening. Word spread about the larger than usual stream of ambulances and heightened activity at Abbeville's station and port, as hospital trains and barges brought in huge numbers of casualties. However, no one knew just how badly the battle was going.

Over the coming days and weeks, the press gave only limited news, vaguely implying the long-planned offensive was going as expected. Even the generals did not at first realise the full scale of the catastrophe. Staff and volunteers at the hospitals suspected the truth about the battle's progress, given the huge swell of casualties overwhelming them.

Yvonne, like everyone else going about their daily business, witnessed soldiers arriving back from the trenches, dazed with exhaustion and changed forever by their experiences. She saw the walking wounded, limping and hobbling, covered in filth and patched with field dressings, ambulances ferrying the more serious casualties to hospital. For the soldiers, coming back to a functioning town with shops, cafés and comfortable beds seemed incredible after the bowels of hell that were the front-line trenches.

Yvonne was also aware of the great number of men departing to the front line, to replace the dead and wounded as the battle wore on. The battle would last until 18 November, eating up young men. The Allies did eventually make progress, pushing the enemy eastwards some distance, but only very slowly and at enormous human cost. Today, the shifting line of the front can be traced on a map by the numerous military cemeteries scattered along its length.

◆ ◆ ◆ ◆ ◆

On 27 July 1916, six weeks after starting work in the Dallon household, and as the Battle of the Somme raged not far away, Yvonne was visited by a social worker, who signed with their initial, 'P'. No other entry on Yvonne's file provides any information about the identity of officials. P reported she was in good health and that Louis Dallon's home was very good and clean. Yvonne had a blanket for her bed and the reciprocal arrangement was deemed satisfactory. P also noted that Yvonne could read and write.

The next inspection six months later, on 12 February 1917, found Yvonne in good health, her bed good and clean with a blanket on it, and all seemed well. The mention of her bed is significant because *domestiques* in the provinces were not always given proper sleeping arrangements, sometimes even having to make do with a roll-out mattress in the corner of the kitchen. The single blanket on Yvonne's bed sounds meagre, insufficient to keep her warm on a cold winter's night in an unheated room, even though it was probably a heavy woollen blanket. She may have slept in her clothes.

The notes on Yvonne's file are perfunctory and there is no mention of the war at any point, or her involvement in the war effort. But there is no doubt Yvonne had to do her bit.

Such was the scale of casualties brought to Abbeville's military hospitals that all the older girls and women of the town were called on to help out, Yvonne among them. Her granddaughter Jan remembers being told that during the war she was 'a schoolgirl who rolled bandages and visited the wounded'. This is not entirely accurate, because she had left school before the outbreak of war in the summer of 1914. However, it is highly likely that after she had left foster care in the summer of 1916, and until the end of the war, she worked as a volunteer in military hospitals. As the Battle of the Somme wore on, extra pairs of hands were desperately needed as

13: THE SHATTERING OF TRANQUILLITY

casualties overwhelmed the hospitals. Yvonne could walk from Monsieur Dallon's house to the British Empire hospitals in the fields on the edge of Abbeville, a distance of three or four kilometres. The British hospital annexe and French military hospitals in town were even closer.

Wherever she was sent, her duties were much the same and brought her to the bedside of wounded soldiers. She would hold a hand, plump up pillows or mop a fevered brow. Witnessing the suffering and the terrible, life-changing injuries would make a lasting and disturbing impression on any young girl. Now Yvonne understood the national hatred for the Germans and considered it justified. Her animosity towards Germany would linger forever.

In the early autumn of 1916, men from Albert Bagley's battalion, the 20th Londons, were doubtless among the casualties arriving at the hospitals in Abbeville. After fighting at Vimy Ridge in April, where the battalion took over from the French, the battalion had been ordered south to the Somme. By late August they were stationed at Brèsle, near Amiens, getting ready to take their turn fighting in the big offensive. In early September they were moved up to the support lines, knowing they would soon be ordered into the front line.

Soldiers spent approximately fifteen per cent of their time in the front lines, rotating with other units, typically for four days at a time, but often longer. Facing the enemy a short distance away over no man's land was terrifying. Worst of all was going over the top during planned attacks, when many were felled by bullets and shells within moments. Harry Patch, the First World War veteran whose story is told in *The Last Fighting Tommy*, explained: '*It doesn't matter how much training you've had, you can't prepare for the reality, the noise, the filth, the uncertainty and the calls for stretcher bearers.*' It took extraordinary bravery and nerve to obey the command, which they did, not least because of their unwavering support for one another. They knew if they gave in to their fear, they helped no one, including themselves.

By Thursday 14 September the 20th Londons were positioned not far from Albert, near Mametz Wood, which had been taken from the Germans in July. They were getting ready to attack. At noon the men were given rum, a clear sign they were about to go into action. Yet the moment did not come immediately. They marched up towards High Wood and waited in nervous suspense, until zero hour eventually came at 6.20 the following morning.

British troops in the Flers-Courcelette area of the Somme, 1916. Albert's battalion fought in this area at High Wood in September 1916

The deadly moment had arrived. Together with other battalions from the London Regiment they advanced on the German positions, but they were held back 'owing to heavy machine gun, rifle and shrapnel fire'. Fierce fighting filled the September morning and by lunchtime, High Wood was in British hands. It was an important victory but it came at devastating cost, with 250 men killed, wounded or missing from the 20th Londons in a single day. For the next two days, the depleted battalion fought on to help drive the Germans back.

Eventually, what was left of the exhausted 20th Londons were relieved by other units, allowing them to regroup and rest. By Saturday 25 September, they were resting in the small village of Millencourt, to the west of Albert and around 19 kilometres away from High Wood. Here, they enjoyed a bath, a rare and very welcome treat.

The respite did not last long. The men were soon back in action on another stretch of the front, east of High Wood. On Friday 1 October they fought in the Battle of Transloy Ridges and on Thursday 7 October were involved in the attacks on the Butte de Warlencourt. Not that the men knew these names at the time. The woods, ridges and patches of the French countryside over which they were ordered to fight all looked much the same and unremarkable.

If Private Albert Bagley was among the casualties of these few weeks

13: THE SHATTERING OF TRANQUILLITY

of intense fighting, there is a good chance he was taken to Abbeville for treatment. The military hospitals at Amiens, though much closer, were doubtless already overflowing. Casualties were often transported long distances on hospital trains and barges to military hospitals near ports, for ease of evacuation across the channel. Some did not survive the journey.

Casualties transported on a hospital train, 1914-18

A Bagley family story suggests Yvonne and Albert first met during the war and this could indeed be true. On volunteer duty in late September or early October 1916, Yvonne could have found herself at Albert's bedside. This is one of two possible time periods when they might have met, although it seems the less likely. At this time, Albert was 18 years old, Yvonne was only fifteen and their time in each other's company could be measured in minutes and hours spread over a limited number of days.

Besides working for Monsieur Dallon, Yvonne helped in a busy hospital perhaps a few afternoons or evenings each week. The wounded did not stay in hospital long because beds were continually needed for new casualties. As soon as possible, the army moved them to a convalescent base on the coast or shipped them home to complete their recovery.

In Albert's case, although he was exhausted, traumatised and very glad to be out of action, his injuries were not grave. His wounds did not end his war. As his service record testifies, he went through to the end. Even if this brief encounter did happen in the autumn of 1916, the chaos of war, the language barrier and Yvonne's subsequent frequent address changes, made it impossible to stay in touch.

Abbeville is mentioned just once in the 20th London's war diary and it is from this period. On 13 September, the day before the troops moved into position at Mametz Wood, the commanding officer wrote: '1.30 pm – First line transport left for Abbeville.' It is not clear what this signifies but may be to do with fetching supplies. This is the only hard evidence that soldiers from the battalion ever went to the town. By 21 October 1916, the part played by Albert's regiment in the Battle of the Somme was over, and they headed north to Flanders, Belgium.

14: Harsh Realities

AFTER A YEAR with Louis Dallon and during one of the wettest summers in living memory, Yvonne, now aged sixteen, left her placement and returned to the hospice in Abbeville. It was July 1917. The reasons why she left the Dallon household are not recorded.

So began a pattern for Yvonne. She did not stay very long in any of her placements and this was quite normal. *Enfants de l'Assistance* often moved around. Either they left a placement of their own accord because they were unhappy or were being mistreated, or the master and mistress sent them away, usually after some disagreement. Rarely were allowances made for any poor behaviour, and putting a toe out of line could mean they were shown the door.

After a few days at the hospice, where she was kept busy, another placement was found for Yvonne. On 2 August 1917 she left Abbeville and travelled to Crécy-en-Ponthieu. An historic old town north of Abbeville, Crécy is famous for an important English victory there in the 14th century, during the Hundred Years' War. The reason why Yvonne was sent away from Abbeville to a town she didn't know is not recorded. The authorities possibly felt she would be safer in Crécy, as the risk of aerial bombardment grew in Abbeville.

Yvonne's new position was at the home of the local mayor, Paul Marie Joseph Thuillier, a 51-year-old farmer from a large local family. The old mairie building where Mayor Thuillier worked still stands, today converted into flats. He lived at or close to 29 rue des Blancs Collets, the main street running through the town, since renamed rue du Maréchal Leclerc de Hauteclocque. (It is quite common for street names to change in France, where it is customary to honour a person who has accomplished great things by naming a street after them.)

Traditionally, the local mayor was the richest and most powerful landholder in the village and for a man in his position, the prestige of having servants was important. Yet the 1911 census shows Mayor Thuillier, a widower, living with his partner Marie and her daughter Ameline, but no servants. The women in the family did the domestic work, consuming all their time. Perhaps the mayor was more interested in saving money than the status symbol of servants. By the time Yvonne joined the household in 1917, Ameline, now aged 27, had left home. The mayor knew an *enfant de l'Assistance* was cheap labour to replace the free labour previously provided by his daughter. It did not prove successful. Yvonne's time with Mayor Thuillier was short-lived.

On 31 October 1917, less than three months after arriving in Crécy, she was sent back to the hospice in Abbeville because of 'insolence and disobedience'. Placing her with the Thuilliers had been ill-advised. Perhaps Madame Thuillier's inexperience with servants caused problems. She was used to running the home with the help of her daughter, and was perhaps too critical and demanding of Yvonne. If Yvonne's behaviour was poor, the root cause was unhappiness. Being uprooted again to live with more strangers had been unsettling. She did not want to be in Crécy, away from the friends she had found in Abbeville and away from the excitement of the military town. Crécy was dull and quiet by comparison.

On her return from Crécy, Yvonne stayed at the hospice more than two weeks, possibly because the nuns needed her help or because of the time it took to find a suitable placement. The Thuilliers, influential people, had not been impressed with her behaviour and her next position needed more careful selection. Yvonne's side of the story counted for nothing, although the kindly but over-worked Sister Jeanne had a sympathetic ear.

It is impossible to know how Yvonne was treated by the people who took her in on the reciprocal scheme. Although some employed an *enfant de l'Assistance* for altruistic reasons, the main attraction was the low cost. Often they cared little for the welfare of the vulnerable young person they employed and just wanted a servant on the cheap. Mistreatment was common, including verbal, psychological and physical abuse, despite some degree of vetting by Assistance Publique before placements were approved.

Inspection visits provided little protection, taking place just once a year unless an employer raised a problem or complaint. Behind closed doors, in the homes of strangers where there was no one to come to her defence, Yvonne was almost certainly exploited or abused in some of her placements. However, even where she was treated fairly, things sometimes went wrong.

❖ ❖ ❖ ❖ ❖

14: HARSH REALITIES

Route Nationale, Pont-Rémy, pre-1914: the Leroy family lived on this road

Yvonne's next placement, happily, was more successful. On 17 November 1917, she left the hospice to begin work for the Leroy family in Pont-Rémy, a small town just south of Abbeville. They lived on Route Nationale and can be found on the 1911 census. The head of the family was Paul Leroy, a miller (*'minotier'*). When Yvonne joined his household he was 56 years old. Paul's wife Marie was 47 and they had two daughters, Marcelle aged 19 and Louise aged 12, and a seven-year-old son, Pierre.

Interestingly, in 1911 they are shown as having two *domestiques*. One of them, Leonie, aged around 19 at the time, was evidently an *enfant de l'Assistance* because in the 'place of birth' column of the census, the word 'hospice' is written. The fact the Leroys had two daughters and previous experience of the reciprocal scheme helps explain why Yvonne's placement with them worked out well. They understood what to expect and treated her kindly. When a social worker visited ten days later to see how Yvonne was settling in, all seemed fine: Yvonne was in good health, had a good clean bed with the required one blanket. The placement was reported to be satisfactory.

Just as in Abbeville, Yvonne was required to do voluntary work for the war effort. This was a regular part of her week. Like every village in the district, Pont-Rémy played its part in the Allied war machine. The railway branch line and the River Somme connected the village easily to Abbeville and beyond. Soldiers were billeted in homes there, possibly even with the Leroy family.

During 1917, a military hospital was set up in Pont-Rémy after it was hastily relocated westwards from Beaumont-Hamel near Thiepval, as the

Germans advanced towards Amiens. It was moved again, just as rapidly, in July 1918, as the Allies pushed the Germans back. So for a period of about eight months from when Yvonne arrived in Pont-Rémy, she probably 'rolled bandages and visited the wounded' in this hospital, within walking distance of the Leroy family home.

The hospital specialised in treating poison gas injuries. By this point in the war, gas shells were regularly deployed by both sides. The hospital's white tents stood in rows on the chalky soil of a hill above Pont-Rémy, not far from Route Nationale, from where there was a magnificent view of the surrounding villages. A Commonwealth War Graves cemetery is located here, the small number of headstones suggesting few patients died of their injuries.[16] The casualties brought to this hospital were mainly British victims of gas attacks. They were very well cared for and in true English style, afternoon tea was served to the patients every day. Yvonne serving tea to Englishmen was a foretaste of a future life she could never have imagined.

If Yvonne did first meet Albert during the war, it seems more likely it was in Pont-Rémy, sometime in late November or December 1917, than in Abbeville in 1916. It is indeed possible that Albert was among the patients at the Pont-Rémy hospital. Records show the 20th Londons fought not very far away during this period, during the Cambrai Operations of late 1917. Cambrai is a town to the north-east of Amiens.

The operations began on 20 November, three days after Yvonne's move to Pont-Rémy, and lasted until 7 December. It was the first offensive of the war when tanks were deployed en masse, to great success for the Allies. Even so, success took many days of bitter fighting and cost huge numbers of casualties on both sides.

The 20th Londons were not the first to fight in the offensive. From 13 to 20 November, they were billeted in the village of Saint Aubin, near Arras, to 'rest', clean their kit, train and generally prepare for further action. On Sunday 18 November they attended church parade and played a football match.

At 11 am on Wednesday 21st, they began the long march towards the Hindenberg Line. In a significant coup, the Allies had recently captured this line of formidable German trench defences. The weather was particularly wet in autumn 1917 and conditions were dreadfully muddy. The men marched for several days in the rain to reach their destination, singing to

---

16 Most of the soldiers buried here died in 1919, and were possibly victims of the flu pandemic while awaiting demobilisation.

14: HARSH REALITIES

keep their spirits up. Old favourites they all knew by heart included 'It's a long way to Tipperary' and 'Pack up your troubles in your old kit bag'.

After arriving in the Hindenberg Line, during the night of the 28th, they were moved up into Bourlon Wood to support the front line. From this point on they were subjected to horrific attacks. Even on the way up to the front line, there were casualties and many more over the coming days as the fighting continued. Enemy fire rained down on them.

When the poison gas shells began bursting around them, those men not already wearing masks reached desperately for them. Masks did not give total protection. The diary entry for 1 December records the battalion suffered around fifty casualties in a 24 hour period, mainly the result of gas. Another forty were recorded the following day. It wasn't until the early hours of 5 December the order came to evacuate the remaining troops from Bourlon Wood and at last they retreated to the relative safety of the Hindenberg Line.

By 6 December, the remaining men of the battalion, spent and despondent, were a safe distance away from the danger zone, regrouping in the village of Bertincourt. They moved on the next day to Havrincourt where they dug new trenches in appalling weather.

There was little time for the depleted battalion to rest. On 11 December they were back in the front line, holding the position. The following day's diary entry records the 'capture of two German prisoners from a hostile patrol.' Over the next few days, they were subjected to enemy fire but there is no mention of further casualties. Mainly the men spent the time trying to improve the state of the rain-filled trenches.

Finally, on 15 December, other units relieved the exhausted and dispirited men. By then, the surviving Bourlon Wood casualties were either in hospital, had been moved to a convalescent base or were on their way home to 'Blighty' (as they called Britain) to complete their recovery.

Was Private Bagley among them? It is impossible to know for sure. If he was, it may have been the poison gas that knocked him out of the battle. The effects of gas were agonising, causing intense irritation to the eyes, ears, nose and throat and in some cases proved fatal.

Wounded soldiers were either rescued from the deafening, deadly chaos going on around them by stretcher-bearers, or, if they could still walk, they weaved their way through the smoke, stench, mud, shell holes, debris, the dead and the dying to the nearest first aid post, a short distance back from the action. Victims of a gas attack, temporarily blinded, were led away to safety in crocodile formation, each man with his hand resting on the shoulder of the soldier in front. The 1919 painting by artist John Singer

Sargent, *Gassed*, depicts this scene. From the first aid post, an ambulance took them to join a hospital train or barge which delivered them onwards to a military hospital, often some distance away. Gas casualties from Bourlon Wood were probably taken to the hospital at Pont-Rémy and the specialist care available there, a distance of 78 kilometres west.

For men lying in pain in a hospital bed, the terrible scenes they had witnessed playing over and over unstoppably in their minds, the fresh face of a pretty young woman turned towards them was the most beautiful sight they had ever seen. Perhaps this is how Albert, 20 years old, felt when 16-year-old Yvonne approached his bedside with a smile. He would never forget her face. They had little time to get to know one another before Albert was moved on, either to complete his recovery or to return to active service.

Hospital barge, 1914-18. The Somme canal was used to transport casualties

In January 1918, the 20th Londons moved further north, seeing more action in the Arras area. During the remainder of the war, the battalion continued to fight in the front line. They fought at Bapaume and on the River Ancre in April 1918, the Battle of Albert in August 1918 and Saint Quentin in September and October 1918, before continuing north to Belgium as the enemy retreated. Yvonne was still living in Pont-Rémy throughout this time, and the military hospital there was dismantled in July 1918. It is less likely Yvonne could have met an injured Private Bagley in this period. However, there were still troops billeted and resting in the

14: HARSH REALITIES

area throughout 1918. On 15 September a log-chopping contest was held at a military forestry camp near Pont-Rémy, in which Australia triumphed over Great Britain, Canada and New Zealand.

In February 1918, Yvonne returned briefly to the hospice in Abbeville suffering from scabies. This is a skin parasitical condition that, though not serious, causes intense itching and is highly infectious. There seems no reason why a doctor couldn't have treated Yvonne where she was. Maybe the Leroys sent her back to the hospice for treatment to reduce the likelihood of anyone else in the household catching it, or because her hands were so badly affected she couldn't work. Certainly, she would have been asked to stay away from the military hospital until she was no longer contagious. She returned to the Leroys on 16 February 1918, when she had recovered. Little did anyone know what a roller-coaster ride the following months would be.

15: Fear and Peace

BEFORE PEACE CAME in November 1918, the civilian population of the Somme suffered the worst terror of the war they had known. Yvonne, still lodging with and working for the Leroy family in Pont-Rémy, was in the thick of it.

In March 1918, the Germans launched their Spring Offensive to attempt a decisive blow. The Americans had declared war in 1917 and the Germans knew it was only a matter of time before the full weight of this took effect. The Spring Offensive was intended to pre-empt this. Taking advantage of the end of hostilities with Russia on the Eastern Front, following the Russian revolution, the Germans redeployed tens of thousands of troops to the Western Front. As the German army pushed westwards, they recaptured Thiepval, the tiny village where Yvonne had spent her earliest years. The ruined village had been held by the British since September 1916.

Fear of invasion was palpable all around. The British began a massive defensive build-up, bringing around 25,000 extra troops into the Abbeville area, which added to civilian speculation about the gravity of the situation. Artillery, heavy and light, was brought in and lined up under the trees, along roads and in the fields. There was incessant movement of troops by road and rail, day and night. As the men headed north to fight, they seemed *'joyeux et fiers'* – joyous and proud – a vestige of morale still holding after nearly four years of war. The scale of activity was extraordinary. Even the tiniest and most obscure village was packed with cannons and troops.

In April, German surveillance planes were seen over Abbeville, assessing the Allied defence preparations, and bombs were dropped on the town. The bombing would continue for four months. The terrified townsfolk took shelter where they could and there were fatalities. The railway station was hit and among other buildings damaged was the hospice on rue George Dumont, where Yvonne had last stayed just a few months earlier, recovering from scabies. The military hospitals on the route de Doullons were also hit.

15: FEAR AND PEACE

Yvonne could not escape the tense, frightened atmosphere. An anti-aircraft gun was put into position in Pont-Rémy, a clear sign of German bombing raids to come. Soldiers flooded into the village. They needed somewhere to stay and households like the Leroys provided billets. No one believed the official line that the extra soldiers had come into the area to 'rest'. Cannons firing in the distance were heard more and more clearly as the enemy approached fast from the east. Yvonne could not mistake the alarm in people's voices as they discussed the situation, weighing up whether to flee, abandoning their homes to pillaging, or take their chances and stay.

At home, she overheard Paul and Marie Leroy talking about it and fretted terribly about what would become of her if they decided to go. Whether they discussed plans directly with Yvonne is debatable. She was an *enfant de l'Assistance* and not their responsibility. Their priority was the safety of their three children, Marcelle, Louise and Pièrre. Yvonne had no one to protect her. Although she may not have realised it, in the chaos ensuing in the event of invasion, Assistance Publique would not be able to come to her aid. Alone, she would have had to bundle up her meagre possessions and join a tide of civilians fleeing south-west on foot, with very little money to survive on. Leaving by train was not an option. The railways were running at full capacity to move troops and the few civilian trains available did not travel far.

Frightening stories had reached the area about the behaviour of German soldiers in the occupied part of France. Their generals instructed them to live off the lands they invaded and take whatever they wanted. This reduced German military supply costs considerably. Consequently, the soldiers looted and stole mercilessly from civilians, who went hungry and cold. Groups of women, children and the elderly were rounded up and sent to concentration camps as hostages and human shields, while teenagers were used for forced labour. There were horrifying tales of rape and summary executions of innocent civilians.

The Allies fought back hard. They knew that Amiens had to be defended at all costs. If the city fell, it would spell disaster. The Allies would lose control of the vital railway junction linking Paris to the Channel ports. Tensions continued to mount as the Germans gained ground. For an intense three-week period in the summer of 1918, the population in and around Abbeville was gripped by fear of imminent mortal danger as the fighting raged on. And then the news improved and with relief, they started to breathe again. The Germans had run out of steam. They had greatly over-stretched their capacity and supply lines and were beginning to crumble on all fronts.

Crucially, the drain the conflict caused on the German economy had destabilised the home front to a dangerous extent. With the population starving, support for the war rapidly fell away. The moment was right for the Allies, under the overall command of French leader Maréchal Foch and strategic direction of the British General Haig, to launch a counter-offensive, which began on 8 August. It caught the Germans by surprise.

The Allies were much better equipped and used the hundreds of tanks at their disposal, more than ever before seen in battle. By contrast, the German army had only a handful of tanks available. Already weakened, they were swiftly pushed back and thousands of German troops were taken prisoner, whole units surrendering in some cases to a single Allied soldier. Many were transported to the Prisoner of War camps at Abbeville.

The Battle of Amiens, as the Allied offensive became known, was the decisive battle of the First World War. Behind the scenes, the German leaders realised defeat was inevitable and started to look for a way to negotiate peace. In the meantime, the exhausted German troops fought on and the slaughter continued.

At 11 am on Monday 11 November 1918, a cold frosty morning on the Western Front, the war at last came to an end. The local population, worn down and dispirited by four years of conflict and the nightmare of being bombed, could hardly believe it was over. Although happy and relieved, their celebrations were muted. People were numbed by the death and destruction so recently visited on their town and the loss of so many Abbeville men over the past four years. The military hospitals in the town were busier than ever, dealing not only with wounded soldiers by this time, but also with those seriously ill with influenza. A new strain of the virus had arrived in France in 1917, brought on American troop ships crossing the Atlantic to join the war. Many soldiers fell dangerously ill on the long voyage.

Little did the Allies realise this particularly deadly strain of the flu would lead to a worldwide pandemic, killing more young men than the war itself. Governments and military leaders failed to heed the warnings of scientists and did not take the threat seriously. Keeping the war machine going at home and abroad took precedence over stopping the spread of the virus. As a result, it rapidly spread out of control among troops, munitions factory workers and everywhere people continued to mix closely together. Young, fit adults were especially susceptible to serious illness and death from the virus. When the pandemic was finally over, it had

15: FEAR AND PEACE

claimed around 50 million lives globally (including Marguerite Poccardi, whom Yvonne knew as a child in Allery). The only continent not affected was Australia, which took the precaution of quarantining all ships before allowing them to dock on Australian shores.

◆ ◆ ◆ ◆ ◆

Yvonne was still in Pont-Rémy, living with the miller Paul Leroy and his family, when she heard the long-awaited news the war was at an end. The household chores still needed to be done that day. As she swept, scrubbed, wrung and chopped, her hands reddening from the work and the cold, she wondered what the future would now hold. Maybe her thoughts turned to her brief encounter with the wounded British soldier who had made her heart beat faster, wondering if Albert had survived and where he now was.

He was almost certainly in Belgium. The 20th Londons ended the war not far from the French border, to the east of Lille. For some months they had been aware the war was turning in the Allies' favour. Recent weeks had brought rumours the Germans were going to ask for an armistice. The cold November night before it came, the battalion was billeted comfortably in private houses in a small village, where the locals welcomed them warmly. The villagers had suffered badly under German occupation and were relieved to have Allied soldiers in their midst.

At 6 am the next morning, the men marched the short distance into the town of Tournai, and this is where they were when the guns fell silent. Poignantly, the battalions War Diary notes simply 'Armistice signed at 11 am.[17] No demonstration'. The men's routine for the day continued much as usual.

The lack of outward jubilation among the troops was not unusual. There were few signs of rejoicing along the Western Front. The men on both sides were totally spent and found it hard to comprehend the war was actually over. The sudden lifting of the ever-present threat of death released the unfamiliar feeling of relief. Slowly, the rigid tension they had held unconsciously for so long began to melt. For the first time in four years, they lifted their eyes beyond the immediate to the future. Most quickly realised they were now out of a job. For those like Albert, underage when they joined up four years previously, army life on active service was all they really knew. Many worried about returning to civilian life and

---

[17] In fact the Armistice was signed around 5am that morning, to take effect at 11am.

would soon discover they were right to be concerned about their employment prospects.

Naturally, thoughts also turned to their fallen comrades who would never go home. Only luck had separated the living from the dead and the survivors wondered what on earth the war had achieved apart from terrible slaughter. Harry Patch summed up the stupidity of it all like this: '*At the end of the war, the peace was settled round a table, so why the hell couldn't they do that at the start, without losing millions of men?*'

By December 1918, Albert's battalion was back in France. They were stationed at Pernes-en-Artois, north-east of Arras in the Pas-de-Calais. Demobilisation in groups was underway by January 1919, but some were made to wait a further five months to return home. Albert's service record suggests he was among the last to be demobbed.

The men were used to long stretches of boredom, which typified the soldier's life away from the perilous excitement of the trenches, but it was a very frustrating time for them. They were exhausted and just wanted to get home to their loved ones. Harry Patch, who had been conscripted into the army, commented: '*It had taken three days to get me into uniform but it would be five months before I got out of khaki and out of the army, and this was to cause a lot of resentment.*'

The army kept the waiting men occupied, often with fairly pointless activities, to prevent order from breaking down. The 20th London's days were filled in a variety of ways. There were sessions of 'educational instruction' intended to help them find employment. There were PT sessions, football and boxing competitions. Church parades were held regularly and there were always 'camp improvements' to be undertaken. Diary entries for April 1919 show they worked on the Pernes military cemetery 'filling in graves etc'. The men also took advantage of plenty of opportunities for a bath. After the filth of the rat-infested trenches, where they went for months covered in lice and unable to wash, this was a wonderful luxury.

Even soldiers on bases in Britain waited a long time to be demobilised. It took time to process each individual. Every soldier had a medical examination before he was issued with papers, according to his entitlement for various benefits. These were generally derisory but intended to ease him back into civilian life.

Eventually, on 4 May 1919, the last of Albert's battalion left Pernes for Le Havre to await embarkation. They sailed for England on 9 May. Albert's army days were over.

16: Mistakes

BACK HOME IN London in the summer of 1919, Albert began the long process of readjustment faced by all returning soldiers. Getting used to life at home after four long years away was difficult for all ex-servicemen. They needed time and space while they tried to settle back into normal life. Not all parents, wives and girlfriends understood this. Well-meaning attempts to reintegrate their men back into family life were sometimes met with an angry and frustrated response. This was bewildering and upsetting for loved ones who only wanted to help.

The economic situation in post-war Britain and employment prospects for ex-servicemen were grim. Few employers had kept jobs open for men who went away to fight and some actively discouraged ex-servicemen from applying for vacant posts. Albert was one of the lucky ones. He found work as a marine clerk. The Bagley family believes he returned to Lloyds of London, where he had been apprenticed prior to joining the army, although there is no surviving evidence to confirm this.

Albert's younger brother had also begun his working days in the shipping industry. Living near the London docks, it was an unsurprising direction for both boys. Records from 1915, held by the National Maritime Museum, list John Gordon Bagley from Woolwich, aged 17, as an apprentice merchant seaman. This career choice spared Gordon, as he was known (avoiding confusion with his father John), from being called up for military service. Yet the work was nonetheless dangerous. Merchant cargo ships played a vital role keeping the nation supplied and fed during the war. They were a constant target for German U-boats and by the end of the war, more than 3,000 British merchant and fishing vessels had been sunk and nearly 15,000 merchant seamen had died.

Resuming the role he had left behind in 1914 was not a success for Albert. Like so many young men who fought in the war, he had changed immeasurably from the boy who left for France. After the dramatic adventure of the war years, pushing a pen behind a desk in an office was a dull daily existence. He couldn't settle and needed to find something new.

❖ ❖ ❖ ❖

Meanwhile, in France, seven months after the Armistice and a month after Albert had returned to England, eighteen-year-old Yvonne left Pont-Rémy and her position with the Leroy family. It was June 1919. She returned to the hospice in Abbeville, this time for several weeks. The reason Yvonne left was not recorded and evidently the Leroys did not dismiss her for any wrongdoing. If she left of her own accord, she was perhaps bored with life in Pont-Rémy which was once again a sleepy backwater after the intense activity of the war years. Abbeville held more attractions for a young woman, and perhaps she was determined to go there, even if it meant waiting for a suitable position to arise.

On 28 June, while Yvonne was at the hospice, the big news story hitting the headlines was the signing of the peace treaty at Versailles. It was the conclusion of six months of negotiations among the world's leaders at a Peace Conference in Paris. The signatories for the Allies were British Prime Minister David Lloyd George, French President George Clemenceau and American President Woodrow Wilson. The news of the signing of the treaty was greeted by the public with jubilation. David Lloyd George received a hero's welcome when he arrived back in London, where the King met him personally as he stepped off the train at Victoria Station.

The Versailles Treaty set out the terms for peace and how much Germany must pay to compensate the Allies for the huge costs of the war. Some felt the treaty should bring Germany completely to its knees, economically and militarily, so the nation could never cause trouble again. Others, including Woodrow Wilson, argued leniency was important for reconciliation and lasting peace in Europe. His view prevailed.

Yet some had serious misgivings. The French commander of the Allies at the end of the war, Maréchal Foch, considered it too lenient. He prophesied the Treaty of Versailles would amount to no more than a 20-year armistice. He was wrong by only 65 days. Even David Lloyd George did not believe the Great War had been the war to end all wars as many hoped. In private he was heard to comment, 'We shall have to do the whole thing over again in twenty-five years' time at three times the cost'.

Leniency had a very subjective interpretation. By the end of the war, Germany was already on its knees, in a state of near-collapse. The nation felt deeply humiliated by the Versailles treaty and thought it far from lenient, amounting to enslavement. It stripped land, assets and military power from the once great nation. Many Germans vowed passionately to make their nation rise again, including a former lance corporal in the

16: MISTAKES

Bavarian army called Adolf Hitler. He was 30 years old when the treaty was signed.

The Treaty of Versailles sowed the seeds of further conflict that would one day have personal repercussions for Yvonne and Albert. But in the summer of 1919, each of them was trying simply to move on with their post-war lives. Albert was safely home with his family in London, attempting to settle back into his job as a marine clerk. Yvonne was very much alone in the Somme, looking for a better future. Three years had passed since she left the shelter and stability provided by the Desjardins. She had grown up fast, learning the hard way it was best to do as she was told if she wanted an easy life.

Naturally, there were times she found this impossible, especially when she felt unfairly treated. And like most *enfants de l'Assistance*, she *was* unfairly treated at times. Certainly, she was left in no doubt the people she served thought her inferior. Unconsciously she began to believe it herself. Feelings of resentment and injustice brewed in her and she would sometimes answer back. With no one else to defend her, she began to stand up for herself.

The war had compounded Yvonne's emotional suffering. There was excitement during those years, yes. But she had also witnessed shocking scenes and knew real fear, both for her safety and for her future. These experiences left a deep impression on her. She had no one to confide in and no family support. Above all she was lonely. She couldn't even turn to Valentine Desjardins because the wartime travel restrictions prevented her from visiting. Around Yvonne's inner insecurities a brittle shell of survival formed. Fortified with this veneer of strength she dreamt of escape from the drudgery of domestic service to a more fulfilling life.

Many young women at this time realised there were now more attractive employment opportunities open to them. The old order was changing in the aftermath of the war. There were new jobs in offices, shops and factories, with conditions regulated by law. These had much more appeal than the long hours, arduous work and lack of leisure time in domestic service (although even as late as 1975 there were still 234,000 people working as *domestiques* in France).

On Yvonne's return to Abbeville, she found it very different from the war years: the military circus had packed up and left town for good. The surviving men had returned home, damaged buildings were being repaired and the Abbevillois were settling back into the humdrum routine of provincial daily life. She spent over six weeks in the hospice where she slotted back into the familiar routine of chores under the direction of the nuns, eating communal meals quietly and sleeping in the dormitory with the other girls. There is no information on her record to indicate why she stayed such a long time in the hospice. She no doubt welcomed the cool of the hospice buildings as it was one of the hottest summers on record.

17. ABBEVILLE - Place de l'Amiral Courbet et Saint-Vulfran

Abbeville in the 1920s: place de l'Amiral Courbet looking towards Saint-Vulfran's church and rue du Pont-aux-Brouettes
Photo courtesy of Archives départmentales de la Somme (France), cote du document 8F12089

Yvonne's next placement began on 9 August 1919. She was sent to 6 rue du Pont-aux-Brouettes, on one of the main commercial streets in the centre of Abbeville, to work for someone by the name of Lemaire. The 19th-century buildings on rue du Pont-aux-Brouettes Yvonne knew no longer exist. They were destroyed in the bombings of World War Two, and the street was reconstructed with modern buildings in the 1950s.

There is no clear evidence to show who made up the Lemaire household Yvonne served. At the time of the 1911 census, there was no-one called Lemaire on rue du Pont-aux-Brouettes. The Abbeville business directory held by the town archives lists a violin teacher called Lemaire at the address in 1918 and by 1919 also a milliner ('*chapellier*') by that name. Like many families trying to make a living, the Lemaires needed more than one string to their bow. Nearly everyone wore a hat in those days, and Lemaire's new shop had plenty of competition in the town, which boasted numerous *chapelliers*.

16: MISTAKES

The Lemaires lived above their shop and Yvonne was taken on as a *bonne*. Her duties would include sweeping the shop floor at the end of the day and generally preparing it for the next morning. If the placement went well, Monsieur Lemaire might also ask her to help behind the counter or even make use of her sewing skills, stitching bows and trimmings onto hat bands. Her new placement felt like a step up in the world. There were certainly opportunities if she managed to make a good impression. Being among the ladies' hats was a great delight. When no one was looking Yvonne could try them on, admiring the effect in the mirror.

The most fashionable designs, especially popular with younger women, were quite different from anything worn in previous times. Narrow brimmed, they fit snug and low on the head, almost concealing the gaze and forcing the wearer to lift her chin and cast down her eyes. The effect was very alluring. First designed in Paris by the milliner Caroline Reboux in 1908, its distinctive bell shape gave the hat its name: '*la cloche*' (the bell).

Colourful cloche hats in felt, sisal and straw were displayed on one side of Lemaire's shop window, catching the eye of women walking along rue du Pont-aux-Brouettes. The 1919 designs fit more snugly than ever, and it was all the rage for women to have their long hair cut short into the cropped style that worked so well with '*la cloche*'. On the other side of the window, the men's flat caps, berets, fedoras and straw boaters, in various shades of grey and beige, excited less attention.

Over the summer of 1919, as the business became more established, the till rang more frequently. Above the shop, Yvonne was occupied during the day with domestic chores in the family's living quarters. When the shop was very busy, Monsieur Lemaire might call up the stairs to Yvonne to drop what she was doing, tie on a fresh white apron and come down to lend a hand. Unfortunately, his trust in her was to be betrayed.

On 14 December 1919, Yvonne was sent back to the hospice for 'bad conduct'. She had been caught stealing 40 Francs. Monsieur Lemaire immediately terminated her placement and reported her to Assistance Publique. Yvonne's file reveals she admitted the theft and returned the money several hours later. There are no clues to her motives for stealing. Maybe there wasn't one. It was just a moment of youthful folly, an unthinking action in an instant of temptation, seeing Lemaire's back turned and an open till at the end of a profitable day. Yvonne had never seen such quantities of cash before and thought a few notes would not be missed.

It was a serious mistake. She was fortunate not to have been reported to the police. 40 Francs was not an insignificant sum, the equivalent of around £50 at today's values.[18] Her confession may have saved her, but also it was the practice of Assistance Publique to keep young people in their care away from the criminal justice system, except in the most serious cases. They particularly did not want *enfants de l'Assistance* ending up in penal institutions, partly because of the corrupting conditions of such places and also because of the cost. It was cheaper to allow Assistance Publique supervisors to discipline and punish misdemeanours themselves.

In Yvonne's case, she received a severe telling off and warning about her future behaviour, before being sent to a new placement. Moving an *enfant de l'Assistance* was a pragmatic way of dealing with incidents like this. Unsurprisingly, Yvonne was sent away from Abbeville, where it was now more difficult to place her. Word would get around about her stealing from the milliner. Given what followed, she must have greatly regretted her actions.

◆ ◆ ◆ ◆ ◆

On Christmas Eve, Yvonne made her way to Bussus-Bussuel, a small agricultural commune of only 280 people, 11 kilometres east of Abbeville. Tucked away in a dimple of the rolling Somme countryside, even today it is a remote location, the population much the same size as in 1919.

Her new employer was the Forestier[19] family. They lived on their farm on rue d'en Haut, a quiet rural lane dotted with farmhouses, each surrounded by its own yard, barn and outbuildings. The Forestier farm was among the largest in the area, occupying land near the centre of the small commune.

In 1911 the head of the household was Paul Forestier (born 1862). He and his wife Berthe (born 1865) lived with their two daughters Nelly (1889) and Thérèse (1893). The family were prosperous enough to employ three *domestiques*: a *cuisinière* and two farmhands. The running of the farm depended on local labour and additional men were hired on a daily basis, the number according to need, which varied depending on the time of year. The Forestiers were significant employers in the village.

The family also had a *'pupille'* living with them at the time of the 1911

---

18 This is a rough estimate. Accurate information about historic currency values is hard to come by. However, it is known that the Franc devalued considerably after the First World War compared to pre-war values.

19 Not their real name.

16: MISTAKES

census. So when eight years later the authorities sought a suitable placement for Yvonne after her misdemeanour in Abbeville, the Forestiers seemed a reasonable choice. They were a respected local family and had experience with *enfants de l'Assistance*. No one knew Yvonne in Bussus-Bussuel and its isolation would help keep her out of trouble.

It is hard to know exactly who made up the Forestier household when Yvonne arrived in December 1919. An indication comes from the 1921 census, which shows two of Paul and Berthe's sons living at the farm. The daughters, Nelly and Thérèse, had left home, perhaps to marry. Strangely, Paul, who lived until 1929, was not recorded at the address.

The wife of one of Paul's nephews still lives in the area and remembers the family were wealthy and owned other properties. Paul was perhaps staying at one of these when the census was taken. She also remembers farming was not their only source of income: Paul held a senior ranking position with the Post Office in Abbeville, which in those days was a very prestigious role. It seems that by 1921, Paul had handed over the running of the farm to his oldest son René (born 1888). He is recorded as the head of the household at the farm in Bussus-Bussuel, living with his mother and his younger brother Jean (born 1895). They employed a *bonne* called Anicet Fournier, who was in her fifties.

There is a good chance this was the household eighteen-year-old Yvonne joined that fateful Christmas in 1919. She was to assist Anicet, serving René aged 31, Jean aged 24 and their 55-year-old mother whose husband was frequently absent. René and Jean had no doubt fought with the French army during the war and were still adjusting to civilian life, including responsibility for the farm.

Yvonne was highly vulnerable to abuse in this isolated set-up and the placement would prove to be one of the lowest points in her young life. While Albert celebrated Christmas 1919 at home with his loving family in London, Yvonne enjoyed no festivities. On the morning she presented herself at the farmhouse door, Berthe and Anicet were already busy in the kitchen, preparing for the traditional Christmas Eve feast. Yvonne was set to work immediately, fetching and carrying to Berthe's commands in the unfamiliar farmhouse.

In the evening as the family sat down to enjoy their festive dinner, a roast goose from their own flock perhaps, Yvonne may not have been invited to join them at the table. More likely she ate leftovers later with Anicet, after they had finished clearing away and washing the dishes. Among strangers once again, Yvonne may have preferred to eat alone. Struggling to mask her dismay and resentment at being banished from Abbeville, and full of self-reproach, she did not want to be with these people, on a farm of all places, stuck in a rural backwater.

Berthe and René would not much like Yvonne's sullen attitude. They neither knew nor cared about her troubles (although would not have accepted her had they known she had stolen money). The inauspicious start set the tone for Yvonne's relationship with the Forestiers. As the wintery days unfolded, the Forestiers' coldness towards her grew while her feelings of dreariness and isolation intensified. Completely cut off from friends she knew in Abbeville, she longed for familiar company and the diversions of the town.

Even the work was harder than she was used to and a far cry from the relative glamour of the hat shop. She was no doubt expected to do chores in the cold, muddy farmyard where her lack of experience around animals and in the dairy invited scornful complaints. The placement felt like punishment for the theft, and probably was.

Peering through the farmhouse windows after nightfall, which was around 5 pm at that time of year, she could barely see a single point of light in the pitch darkness outside. After her work was finished for the day, Yvonne had nothing to occupy her, nowhere to go and only Anicet for company. She went to bed early, huddling under the blanket to keep warm, and cried at the unfairness of it all. The murmur of René, Jean and Berthe's voices could be heard downstairs as they talked around the fire into the evening, then their movements as they came up to bed, until finally the house was quiet. The silence was broken only by the howl of the wind, bestial noises from the barn or the creak of a bedroom door.

❖ ❖ ❖ ❖ ❖

A month later, Yvonne could bear it no longer. She ran away. Yvonne's file offers no clues as to what triggered such drastic action. Reading between the lines, something bad happened, a row perhaps with Berthe, or unwanted advances from René or his younger brother Jean – or worse. Young girls in Yvonne's situation, working as *bonnes* on isolated farms, were considered easy prey by unscrupulous masters, particularly if they were *enfants de l'Assistance*. Such men knew they could get away with it. They would never be confronted by the girl's angry father or brother.

Yvonne waited for Sunday, her day off, when she was free to go out and would not draw attention. The weather was exceptionally mild for the time of year and Yvonne picked her way along the rutted lanes of Bussus-Bussuel, avoiding the puddles, until she reached the main route to Abbeville.

16: MISTAKES

There, she could wait for a bus to take her into the town, then catch a local train on the southbound line. In her distress, she knew instinctively where to go. Her file records that on 25 January 1920 she was 'in Allery with her former foster mother.' She had returned to Valentine.

Yvonne had stayed in touch with the Desjardins and friends in Allery as best she could in the years since she had left, although it was not easy to do so. During the war years, civilian travel restrictions made visiting Allery very difficult, impossible even. Although the first telephones had arrived in Abbeville as early as 1899, neither Yvonne nor the Desjardins, poor people in a rural location, had access to one. Perhaps Yvonne wrote to Valentine occasionally to let her know where she was and how she was doing.

After the war ended, Yvonne naturally headed 'home' when she could, drawn by the comfort of the familiar and the people who were her 'family'. By 1920, she could travel freely but the ease with which she could visit Allery depended on where she was living, how much free time she had and what she could afford.

From Bussus-Bussuel the journey to Allery took more than an hour and cost the price of a bus and a train ticket. Yvonne had no way of warning Valentine she was coming, but it was not unusual for Valentine to find Yvonne on her doorstep on a Sunday. She was, however, surprised and concerned at her obvious distress.

Yvonne's decision to flee to the Desjardins lends weight to the possibility that something dramatic happened on the lonely farm in Bussus-Bussuel. If it was simply that she wanted another placement, she would have presented herself at the hospice to ask for one. Her actions also reveal the kind of relationship she had with Valentine and Alfred. Three and a half years after leaving their care, Yvonne still felt able to turn to them in a crisis.

Valentine knew she must tell the authorities as soon as possible where Yvonne was. After calming her and settling her by the warmth of the stove, she agreed she could stay the night. The next morning, a Monday, Valentine put on her coat and set off for the mairie, where staff telephoned Assistance Publique to report what had happened. For reasons that are not recorded, Yvonne was allowed to stay with the Desjardins for six days. Again, this points to something dark happening to Yvonne at the Forestier farm. Why else would she have stayed with the Desjardins for nearly a week if not because she was so upset that she needed their support?

Valentine was in a difficult position. Yvonne was no longer her responsibility and at the time she had more foster children under her roof (the following year's census shows two children in the Desjardins' care). Nonetheless, she allowed Yvonne to stay and liaised with Assistance Publique on her behalf. Eventually, Yvonne was instructed to report to Hospice Saint-Charles in Amiens, a disappointment to her, as she wanted to stay close to 'home'. It was still too soon after the theft from the hat shop for her to return to the Abbeville area. The authorities were also keen to keep her away from Valentine, whom they were paying to look after her current foster children. It was not appropriate for her to concern herself with a girl who had moved on from her care years earlier.

Yvonne made her way to Amiens the following Saturday, 31 January 1920. Unlike the hospice in Abbeville, Yvonne was unfamiliar with the hospice Saint-Charles. She had been too young to remember the last time she had crossed its threshold, although she was aware she had spent time there as a young child.

It had been a challenging period for Yvonne since leaving the Leroys in Pont-Rémy the previous summer. Her disgrace in Abbeville and the bad experience in Bussus-Bussuel compounded the cumulative effects of the trauma of the war, loneliness and emotional deprivation. She was a troubled 18-year-old and like many young people in her circumstances, was becoming more rebellious. She resented the control social workers had over her life and the demeaning placements they found for her. After all, she had been independent in many ways since leaving foster care and felt capable of making her own decisions. In truth, however, she was still highly vulnerable. Inadequate and impersonal though it was, Assistance Publique was Yvonne's only guaranteed source of protection and support, and was better than nothing. She did not appreciate this at the time.

It is no wonder that Yvonne was unhappy and unsettled. From the age of 15, in the middle of the war, she had been uprooted from her secure life in Allery, moved around between towns and villages, been in and out of hospices and forced to live with strangers who were not always kind and were sometimes cruel. She repeatedly had to adjust to new circumstances. It was confusing, disorientating and dispiriting. Yvonne belonged nowhere.

Living under the same roof as the families she served, but set apart from them, she felt isolated and on edge, always fearful of doing or saying something that would provoke their scorn. She missed dreadfully the safe, familiar feeling of being part of the Desjardins family and longed to go home, although of course she knew that for her, in reality, no such place existed. Her true family background was a complete mystery to her and naturally she wondered endlessly who her family were, what they looked

16: MISTAKES

like, how they spoke and where they were now. Dreams of finding a birth family who would welcome her with open arms were tempered by painful thoughts about her mother. Why did she abandon her? Was she still alive? These questions would haunt Yvonne her whole life.

❖ ❖ ❖ ❖ ❖ ❖

A few days after Yvonne arrived at Hospice Saint-Charles, a new placement was found for her in Amiens. On Tuesday 3 February 1920, Yvonne knocked on the door of 57 rue Louis Thuillier to report to her new mistress. The quiet residential street where she lived runs parallel to rue Saint-Fuscien, about a mile south of the city centre, where today the Somme Archive facility is located.

Rue Louis Thuillier has changed little over the past century. Terraced houses of moderate proportions line the narrow street, their front doors opening directly onto the pavement. Number 57 is at the end of a respectable, orderly row of homes built in red brick, offset with pale mortar, each with a pair of shuttered windows on the ground and first floors. On the third floor was the attic room where Yvonne would sleep, its large dormer window dominating the roofline and offering a good view over the rooftops of the neighbourhood.

Outhouses in the back garden included a toilet. There was no indoor bathroom and this was quite normal for the times. At home with the Desjardins and in some of her placements, Yvonne might have use of a tin bath with hot water once a week. Otherwise, she used the public bath house. In many towns, including Amiens, this was owned and run by the philanthropic savings bank, Caisse Épargne. This was the same bank which held the savings account opened for Yvonne by Assistance Publique when she entered domestic service at the age of fifteen.

Yvonne's new employer was 84-year-old Esther Magnier. Born in 1839, she appears on the 1911 census at 57 rue Louis Thuillier living with a friend 20 years her junior, Mathilde Pourchelle. This was possibly two widows or spinsters sharing a home, with the younger woman looking after her older friend. When Yvonne arrived nine years later, Esther may have been living there alone, explaining her need for a *bonne*. Assistance Publique perhaps reasoned Yvonne would be safe living under the roof of an elderly widow, after what had happened on the Forestier farm. Little account was taken of how Madame Magnier might treat Yvonne and whether she was suitable to take on a vulnerable 18-year-old girl in desperate need of kindness. Placements were not always easy to find.

57 rue Louis Thuillier, Amiens, today

There was drama just two days after Yvonne's arrival. The record reveals she turned up at the hospice on Thursday 5 February but later the same day was again at Esther Magnier's home. This suggests Yvonne walked out on her new position and was immediately sent back. Perhaps Yvonne took exception to the way Madame Magnier spoke to her and found her impossible to please. Staff at the hospice had little sympathy and insisted Yvonne must continue with the placement. She had no alternative. Yvonne returned to face Madame Magnier's wrath with a heavy heart, feeling lonelier and more miserable than ever.

17: 'A Good Girl at Heart'

A SHORT TIME later in England, Albert, now aged 22, was embarking on a new career. On 1 March 1920, he joined the Metropolitan Police. His service record states his former occupation as 'marine clerk' but does not confirm the name of his employer. Albert had not adjusted to regular days sitting behind a desk after life in the army. The police force offered more interest for an ex-soldier and good job security.

After a short period of initial training, he was posted with 'A' Division, based at Canon Row Police Station in Central London. This gave him the chance to move out of the family home in Blackheath (where they lived until at least 1935) because there were living quarters for single men at the station itself.

Officers from 'A' Division on duty, Downing Street, c.1921

The red brick buildings of Canon Row Police Station formed part of the famous New Scotland Yard building designed by the architect Norman Shaw. It opened in 1902 and for ninety years it was one of the Metropolitan Police's most important stations, until they moved operations to Charing Cross in 1992. Situated in the heart of Whitehall, officers from Canon Row policed all London's major political and royal events in the

20th century. Officers standing guard outside number 10 Downing Street came from Canon Row.

Albert was assigned warrant number 109345 and issued with his uniform. The dark single-breasted tunic he wore fastened from neck to waist with eight shiny metallic buttons. Beneath a belt around his middle, the tunic had no fastenings, allowing ease of movement when chasing after criminals. The mandarin-style stand-up collar bore the characters A783, denoting Albert's unique officer number. His kit included an electric lantern, very recently introduced to replace the oil lamps previously issued to officers. He took up boxing again around this time and was a runner-up in a Metropolitan Police championship.

✦ ✦ ✦ ✦ ✦

While Albert was getting used to being back in uniform in the spring of 1920, albeit a police uniform this time, Yvonne was still working for Madame Magnier in Amiens. She was deeply unhappy.

A social worker visited on 7 June 1920, four months into Yvonne's placement, and recorded her 'conduct leaves something to be desired' and she has a 'strange character' ('*bizarre de charactère*'). No details are given about the less than desirable conduct or what prompted Esther Magnier to describe Yvonne as strange. Yvonne was miserable and lonely stuck in the house at the beck and call all day of a demanding old lady, who found her sullen and inclined to answer back.

Behind Yvonne's outward demeanour lay a growing catalogue of trauma, most recently the trouble in Bussus-Bussuel a few months previously. She had no one to talk to about how she was feeling and no one cared enough to ask. Her only escape was to go looking for fun and diversion with people her own age in her free time.

Amiens was still being rebuilt after the destruction of the war but there were cafés, bars and dances open where young people socialised. Craving affection, Yvonne was susceptible to any man paying her attention. Madame Magnier would be concerned about the company her *bonne* kept and the time she returned after a night out. Complaints about Yvonne staying out late were to surface repeatedly during subsequent placements.

Yvonne was free to go out in the evening if she wished. Conditions were improving for *domestiques* by 1920 after years of growing protests about poor working conditions and long working hours. Progress had been slow. It was a struggle for *domestiques* to band together to force change. The very nature of the work meant they led isolated lives with little time

17: 'A GOOD GIRL AT HEART'

off. Annual leave entitlement was unheard of. At best, a *domestique* might be granted a few days' unpaid leave to visit a sick or dying parent.

Gradually the demand for change gathered momentum and their voices began to be heard, backed by social reformers. It was a phenomenon seen in many countries, including Britain and America. In Australia in April 1907, domestic servants issued an ultimatum, demanding a 12-hour day including two hours of breaks, a finishing time no later than 8.30 pm and 2 pm on Thursdays and Sundays, plus eight days' holiday a year. Very modest demands by today's standards. In Russia, the 1917 revolution brought dramatic and rapid change for workers' rights. In postwar France, the regulation of domestic service was strengthened, giving *domestiques* equivalent rights to other workers. While Yvonne remained in the care of the state, officials were responsible for ensuring her employers abided by the law, even though enforcement was in practice difficult.

Madame Magnier, despite her complaint, showed some sympathy for Yvonne: she did not send her away. Rather the social worker, seeing how unhappy Yvonne was, realised the placement was not suitable and a new one should be found. They specified she should not be placed anywhere in 'Amiens town, nor in the Allery region, nor in Abbeville town'. There are a few possible reasons for this.

The social worker was concerned about the temptations and bad influences in town having a negative effect on Yvonne's behaviour. Yvonne may have asked for a placement in Allery to be close to Valentine, but the authorities wanted to keep her away from her former foster home. They frowned on the support Valentine gave when Yvonne had fled there from Bussus-Bussuel. The needs of the foster children currently in her care had to come first. In an effort to return Yvonne to the straight and narrow, a fresh start somewhere new was prescribed.

Four days after the social worker's visit, Yvonne left the house on rue Louis Thuillier for the last time and returned to Hospice Saint-Charles. The date was 11 June 1920, her 19th birthday. With no one to wish her a '*joyeux anniversaire*' (happy birthday), saying '*adieu*' to Madame Magnier was Yvonne's only celebration that day.

After a few days in the hospice, on 16 June 1920, Yvonne began a new placement with a family by the name of Ricaut. They ran a hardware store and ironmongers in the village of Airaines, just four kilometres from Allery. This was a welcome compromise for Yvonne. Someone at Assistance Publique had taken a gentler view. She could walk from Airaines to Allery, enabling her to see the Desjardins and her childhood Allery friends, at least occasionally.

The Ricaut household were listed on the following year's census. There was Maurice aged 43, his wife Martine, 40, their sixteen-year-old daughter Audrey and a female *'employée de commerce'* (business employee) called Lea Lebrun who was twenty-eight. Yvonne's name also appears on the census beneath Lea, her profession listed as *'domestique'*. Her place of birth was recorded as Amiens; however, this information was not provided with any certainty and was of course incorrect.

A simple question like 'where were you born?' was difficult for Yvonne. She didn't know the answer. Such questions were another reminder she was different from other people. At this point in her life, Yvonne could say very little about her origins. At most, she knew she had been taken from the hospice in Amiens as a small child to live with the Desjardins. Perhaps this is how she answered Maurice as he completed the census form. As head of the household, he was responsible for the census return and did not want to leave the space blank against Yvonne's name in the column headed *'Lieu de naissance'* (place of birth). Yet for Yvonne, her place of birth was a blank, a black hole where there should have been firm ground.

Maurice Ricaut & Co. was a substantial business. The shop stood on a prominent corner plot in the main market square, place Henri Fissot. A photo taken before the Great War shows a couple examining the oil lamps, jugs, platters and other household goods abundantly displayed in the shop window. It was evidently a well-established, thriving concern which had expanded over the years.

The Ricaut's hardware shop, Airaines, pre-1914

17: 'A GOOD GIRL AT HEART'

The shop occupied the ground and first floors of the building on the corner and extended into the ground floor of an adjacent building facing the square, where the shop entrance was located. The family lived above this part of the shop, with Yvonne and Lea sleeping in the attic rooms on the second floor. From the dormer windows, when her working day was done, Yvonne could see anything happening in the market square. The shop and indeed place Henri Fissot where it stood no longer exist, destroyed when Airaines was bombed in the Second World War.

Yvonne's job, as usual, was to do the household chores. Other duties would include sweeping the shop floor and cleaning its windows. Lea was specifically employed to work in the shop and mainly helped Maurice behind the counter. Maurice and Martine's teenage daughter Audrey no doubt also lent a hand although the census states she was *'sans profession'* (not employed).

Yvonne had been given a second chance with this placement. Assistance Publique had decided to show trust in her in the hope she would respond well and become more settled. Even though she was employed as a *bonne*, if she made a favourable impression there might be a chance to gain shop work experience. It might even be a route out of domestic service for her.

Regardless of the opportunity presented, Yvonne's pattern of behaviour continued. A note on her file in March 1921 says Yvonne 'is a fantastic character, a good girl at heart, has learnt to be a dressmaker, enjoys her placement' but also that her conduct is 'loose', that she 'goes dancing and comes back at 3 am, it is impossible to stop her, or else she sulks, neglects her work and threatens to leave her position immediately.' There is no information about where Yvonne was going dancing until the early hours or who with. There was not much nightlife in Airaines, and Abbeville was 20 kilometres away. Possibly she spent time with her old friends Louis and Sosthène in neighbouring Allery.

It was while Yvonne was working for the Ricaut family in Airaines that she received devastating news. On 4 May 1921, Valentine Desjardins died at home on chemin de Mérélessart, at the age of just 45. Alfred had the painful task of registering her death and his signature appears on the death register. The cause of death was not recorded.

Yvonne was 19 years old. Losing the only person in all the world she was truly close to, the woman she thought of as 'mother', was a terrible blow. Alfred, grieving for his wife and preoccupied with sorting out arrangements for the current foster children under his roof, was unable to offer much comfort. Yvonne may have turned for solace to 'Madame

Charlotte', the Desjardins' neighbour and mother of her childhood friend Jeanne, who had always treated her kindly.

Soon afterwards, for reasons that are not recorded, Yvonne left her position with the Ricaut family after nearly a year in Airaines. On 30 May 1921, she returned again to the hospice in Amiens.

❖ ❖ ❖ ❖ ❖

A further placement was quickly found for Yvonne and this time she was allowed to stay in Amiens again. She started work in the home of Doctor Léon Dubois, at 10 boulevard de Belfort, on 1 June 1921. A census had just recently been completed and shows who was living in the Dubois household.

Doctor Dubois was aged 43 and a respectable professional. An ear, nose and throat specialist, he had qualified in Lille in 1907.[20] He lived with his 40-year-old wife Madeleine and their five-year-old son Pierre. The family were well-to-do, their home a spacious apartment in one of the 19th-century bourgeois apartment buildings along boulevard de Belfort. This was a wide cobbled street not far from the railway station, one of the main thoroughfares encircling the city centre. Although some of the 19th-century buildings still remain today, a modern block now stands on the site of number 10.

It was a well-chosen placement for Yvonne, where she had the chance to settle in the home of decent people who treated her fairly. She told a social worker she enjoyed working for Doctor and Madame Dubois. However, she was now living very close to the city centre and again felt the pull of its attractions and temptations. Her old behaviour continued, stretching the goodwill of the doctor and his wife.

It is hardly surprising that Yvonne wanted to go out, have some fun and look for romance, just like any 20-year-old. For her, there was also a huge void of affection to be filled. This made her vulnerable when it came to the opposite sex. She had neither the protection nor the restraining hand of parents or older siblings, as any man she met would quickly become aware. Her nights were once more spent in the cafés, bars and dance halls of Amiens, just as during her ill-fated placement with Madame Magnier the previous year. She was free to pick up where she left off with acquaintances, perhaps mixing with people the doctor might consider the wrong crowd, and stayed out very late. It cost her the placement.

20 According to the 'Annuaires du département de la Somme'.

17: 'A GOOD GIRL AT HEART'

A note on Yvonne's file dated 14 September 1921 records Yvonne 'goes out in the evening and comes back late in the night'. Yvonne, emerging from her attic room late for duty in the morning, bleary-eyed and yawning, would be summoned immediately by the doctor or his wife for a stern ticking-off. When Yvonne's behaviour failed to improve despite repeated warnings, Doctor Dubois sent her away. Yvonne had blown another good placement and the fresh chance she had been given in Amiens. She returned in disgrace to the hospice, this time in Abbeville.

❖ ❖ ❖ ❖ ❖

Two months passed. This was the longest spell Yvonne ever spent in a hospice. Worried social workers were unsure where to place her next. Conscious she had only nine months' support from them remaining, it was crucial her final placements were a success. The nuns kept her busy at the hospice and she settled into its familiar routine of daily life, under the watchful eye of the nuns. Sister Jeanne in particular, who had great reserves of compassion, would counsel girls like Yvonne, whose behaviour put them at risk. One serious concern was that she would fall pregnant, setting in train another cycle of poverty, abandonment and emotional deprivation. She was in danger of repeating the pattern of her mother's life. The nuns prayed this would not happen.

Eventually, Yvonne was sent to a new placement. She wanted to stay in Abbeville, which she considered her home town, and was allowed to do so. Social workers and the nuns impressed on her the need for good behaviour and conformity as she prepared for independence. Ready to move on from the regimented routine at the hospice, Yvonne promised she had learnt her lesson and had changed.

On Wednesday 17 November 1921, Yvonne knocked on the door at 4 rue Dumont, just along the street from the hospice, to begin her next placement. Again she had to live among strangers in another new household. This time her employers were the Raymond family. The head of the household was 60-year-old Marie Octave Raymond. He lived with his 53-year-old wife Hélène and their children, 19-year-old Robert and 17-year-old Marcelle. At the time of the census earlier that year, they also had a 15-year-old *bonne* called Virginie living with them. Yvonne was perhaps hired to replace Virginie after she moved on.

Yvonne was not the only new arrival at the Raymonds' home that week. Someone placed a small ad in the local paper, *Le Pilote de la Somme*, on

Friday 19 November, appealing for the owner of a homing pigeon to come forward and claim it. The bird was roosting uninvited at 4 rue Dumont.

A note on Yvonne's file dated 1 December 1921 records she was authorised to keep all of her first month's salary to pay the dentist. This required special permission because normally Assistance Publique retained a portion of her wages to pay into her savings account.

Yvonne only stayed with the Raymonds for six months, although there is no indication anything had gone wrong with the placement. It seems Yvonne had simply found a better-paid position for herself. There was no need for her to return to the hospice in between placements this time. Nothing on her file in this period suggests there were any concerns about her behaviour. She had matured enough to finally understand she must conform to the behaviour expected of her if she wanted to get on in life. In little more than six months' time, she would leave the care of Assistance Publique and be completely independent. In future, she would have to find her own employment. She would need good references to survive.

Her new position was with a retired couple who lived just around the corner from the Raymonds, at 35 rue Millevoye. She moved there on 1 May 1922, six weeks before her 21st birthday. The 1921 census records Anatole Mouret, aged 73, at this address, together with his 65-year-old wife Martine and their 30-year-old son Paul, a clerk. Anatole Mouret was a '*rentier*' – in other words, he was retired with his own private means or pension.

A note in the margin of Yvonne's file shows she received 12 Francs a month wages from Monsieur Mouret, in addition to her board and lodgings. This was paltry in the extreme, especially when compared to the 50 Francs a month her mother Marie could earn as a *cuisinière* in Paris twenty years previously. The meanness of Yvonne's pay reflected her status as an *enfant de l'Assistance* working as a *bonne* in the provinces. As usual, she was engaged on a casual basis only ('*sans contract*') and she had no job security whatsoever. This was her immediate future on leaving the protection of Assistance Publique. The notes made on 1 May 1922 were the last on her file before it was closed just six weeks later.

The story of Yvonne's time in the care of the Department of the Somme is sandwiched between pages of similar records for dozens of other *enfants de l'Assistance* in the early part of the 20th century. The volume rested on a shelf in an Assistance Publique office among hundreds of identical volumes documenting the painful childhoods of countless more. An official took down the volume and turned to Yvonne's pages one final time the following year to finalise the bureaucracy. After that, the notes, scribbled

17: 'A GOOD GIRL AT HEART'

by numerous busy social workers who dealt with Yvonne between 1905 and 1921, did not see the light of day for nearly 100 years.

Barely 10 months after leaving the care of Assistance Publique, Yvonne was married and already expecting her first child.

Part Five: Independence and Marriage, June 1922 onwards

18: Freedom and Trepidation

1922 WAS A pivotal year in Yvonne's life, when her fortunes began to change. She turned twenty-one on 11 June and was released from the care of the state. From now on she must make her own decisions with no one at all to guide or support her. She missed Valentine more than ever. With independence came a sense of trepidation but also freedom and opportunity. Four years on from the end of the war, the world seemed full of new possibilities for young people, even those from disadvantaged backgrounds like Yvonne. It was a time when many looked forward with hope and tried to forget the past.

Waves of a new kind of artistic expression were sweeping major cities on both sides of the Atlantic. In America, the Roaring Twenties were underway, while in France the era was called the *Années Folles* (the 'crazy years'). Heady excitement shook Paris with a wild energy that rippled out towards the provinces, where it was felt only as a slight tremble. In the cafés and bars of Abbeville, the regulars sipped coffee and pastis to the strains of Maurice Chevalier singing his hit 'Pas pour moi' ('Not for me'), playing low on the wireless in the background.

At public dances in the town, couples still waltzed and foxtrotted across the floor, unaware they would soon be eagerly practising the steps of a radically new kind of dance. It didn't involve holding your partner close in a traditional upright stance. Instead, it was performed with individual abandon, loose-limbed and free-spirited. This dance eventually became known as the Charleston after the hit tune of the same name by American composer James P. Johnson.

In the growing atmosphere of optimism, Yvonne dared to believe she could leave behind the loneliness and drudgery of domestic service and move up in the world with more attractive and better-paid work. A job in a dress shop would suit her perfectly.

◆ ◆ ◆ ◆ ◆

A few months earlier in London, 24-year-old Albert had left the Metro-

18: FREEDOM AND TREPIDATION

politan Police. He resigned of his own accord on 27 January 1922, and it was, on the face of it, a surprising decision. Although wages for constables were low at this time, the police service offered job security at a time of high unemployment, particularly among ex-servicemen. Post-war unemployment peaked in 1921. Albert told his family he had resigned out of frustration. He wanted to work in the CID and maintained he was effectively barred because he was not a Freemason. The records held by the Metropolitan Police Archives indicate this was at best only part of the story. His service record on leaving rates his overall conduct as 'good'. This is a rather reserved assessment and there is evidence to suggest why he did not receive a more glowing reference.

In June 2018, Albert's war medals were sold in an online auction for £125 (the seller unknown). Information relating to the sale showed Albert received the three medals awarded to servicemen who served for the duration of the war, the 1914-15 Star, the British War Medal 1914-18 and the Allied Victory Medal. All were inscribed with his name and service number. The medal trio were popularly known as Pip, Squeak and Wilfred after cartoon characters in a popular comic strip published in the *Daily Mirror* newspaper in the 1920s. The description of the auction lot gave a short resume of Albert's army and police service and includes the claim that he was '*severely reprimanded and strictly cautioned and fined in March 1921*'. Records in the Metropolitan Police Archives confirm this and show Albert was in trouble again nine months later. The second occasion was on 3 January 1922 when he was docked three days' pay, 'to be extended over three weeks', with his conduct to be reviewed again three months later. He handed in his notice before this review could take place.

The nature of his misconduct is not recorded either time; however, it is unlikely it was as serious as the punishment suggests. Police orders from this period show many officers received reprimands and punishments, often for trivial offences. This reflects general discord at the time. Immediately after the war, rank and file officers began demanding better pay and conditions, and the right to form a union. With troubled ex-servicemen in the workforce and revolution still in the air abroad, it is not surprising commanding officers enforced stringent discipline with harsh punishments.

Canon Row police station was just off Whitehall, where the Cenotaph stands. The Cenotaph was designed by Sir Edward Lutyens, who went on to design the Thiepval Memorial. It was unveiled on 11 November 1920, as a permanent memorial in Portland stone to those who had fallen in the Great War, replacing a temporary structure erected for a peace parade in the war's immediate aftermath. Albert's division policed the very first Remembrance services there, held on Armistice Day, a moving experience for any ex-soldier who had fought in the conflict. They wanted to forget, not remember.

Unveiling of the Cenotaph and the Funeral of the Unknown Warrior, Armistice Day, 1920. 'The Great Silence'. (©IWM)

Albert saw the Cenotaph every time he placed his helmet on his head and set out from the police station to go on patrol. It was a constant reminder of what he had been through. However, it was not reminders of the war that prompted Albert's resignation. What he did next testifies to that. Perhaps he found, after all, he'd had enough of being in uniform. The quasi-military discipline of the police service at times seemed petty and frustrating after the years serving on the Western Front. It was a difficult adjustment for an ex-serviceman still coming to terms with his experiences. This possibly explains why his commanding officers had cause to reprimand him.

Apart from Albert's family, someone else deserved an explanation for his decision to give up a secure job: his fiancée Patricia. It is not clear when they met or how long they had been engaged. Albert's sister Catherine recalled he had been engaged to another girl called Jessie before asking Patricia to marry him. Tall, dark and handsome, Albert no doubt had plenty of admirers. In 1922 Patricia had an engagement ring on her

18: FREEDOM AND TREPIDATION

finger and was looking forward to their wedding. She was perturbed by Albert's decision to leave the police and what it meant. She could not have guessed what the coming months would bring.

19: Daring to Dream

IN THE SUMMER of 1922, as Yvonne contemplated her future, she dreamt about more than getting out of domestic service. Most girls in her situation longed for a man to settle down with and ideally marry, a good man who would support her and provide a proper home in which they would raise a family together. It was not only Yvonne's wish that she should marry. As far as the state was concerned, the marriage of an *enfant de l'Assistance* was an excellent outcome of their programme of intervention, a real mark of success. The state's policies were designed to mould children like Yvonne into independent adults who settled down and contributed to the success of the nation. If she became a wife and mother, producing children to help swell the population, Assistance Publique could congratulate itself for doing a good job.

Yvonne was raised in a family environment, because the state realised not only was this cheaper than an institution, it was more effective. It was undoubtedly better for her well-being, although this wasn't true in all cases. Yvonne had good foster parents and in this respect she was more fortunate than many. Valentine and Alfred Desjardins gave her stability and a relatively normal childhood for twelve of her most formative years. But love? With a number of children passing through their care, this is something they could not freely give. For all their sakes, they kept some detachment from the children temporarily in their lives. When the bond of love is absent, a child's emotional development is deeply affected.

The Desjardins did care for Yvonne diligently, with kindness, and were evidently fond of her. This foundation had helped her weather the storms of the six years that followed, when between the ages of 15 and 21 she moved placements nine times, lived in six different towns and villages, and was admitted to the hospice, either at Abbeville or Amiens, on eleven occasions. During these turbulent years, when at times she was unkindly treated or abused, she became increasingly unhappy, her behaviour sometimes defiant and unwise. These were symptoms of a young girl struggling to cope emotionally with her experiences without the support of family.

19: DARING TO DREAM

During this period she remained in touch with Valentine and Alfred as best she could. They had been a vital, if thin, lifeline of moral support. The couple could do little more than offer Yvonne encouraging words because they were busy caring for the next in the line of abandoned children raised under their roof. At the time of the 1921 census, shortly before Valentine passed away, she and Alfred were fostering an eleven-year-old girl, Léonie, and a three-year-old boy, Robert. Still living in Allery, they had moved to rue du Quayet, on the other side of the crossroads from chemin de Mérélessart. Perhaps by now, they could afford to rent a more comfortable home. The start Valentine and Alfred gave Yvonne was just about enough. It is surely in no small part down to their parenting skills that Yvonne was eventually capable of sustaining a long marriage and raising a family, even if she struggled at times in her roles as wife and mother.

The state had also given Yvonne a basic education and made sure she learnt some skills – domestic work and sewing – to enable her to earn a living. Yvonne's file includes a document, dated June 1922, showing the final act of state care. It authorised her to receive a dowry of the savings accumulated for her since the age of 15 when she left foster care. It amounted to 1,326 Francs and 46 centimes, the equivalent of around £1,650 today.[21] Assistance Publique advised her to use it wisely.

---

21 Rough estimate. Reliable historic conversion information is hard to find.

20. Encounter

SOMETIME DURING 1922, Yvonne and Albert met. It is impossible to say with complete certainty they met *again*. If they did have a brief encounter in a military hospital five or six years earlier, this raises many questions. Had they somehow stayed in touch in the intervening years? The difficulty this would have posed makes it improbable. The only means of staying in contact was by letter. During a brief stay in a hospital, Albert could have given Yvonne his home address in London and asked her to write. The postal system from Britain to soldiers overseas was very reliable. Letter writing was actively encouraged by the military and the Government, who realised the importance of regular contact from home to troop morale. Albert's parents could forward letters arriving for him at the family home to wherever he was, via the army.

However, even if Albert received letters from Yvonne, the chances of his replies reaching her were slim. She moved address many times between 1916 and 1922. A letter delivered for Yvonne after she had moved on from a placement is unlikely to have reached her. Former employers would not have bothered to track her down, particularly if they had sent her away for some misdemeanour. What is more, Yvonne could not understand English and it would have tested Albert's French to keep correspondence with her going for years as she moved around her placements. He doubtless learnt some French at school and many British soldiers picked up the language during their years in France and Belgium. Billeted behind the lines in nearby towns and villages, it was helpful to be able to converse a little with the locals. Speaking a bit of French to get by was one thing, but Albert had less cause to practise reading and writing in the language.

Could Yvonne and Albert, both so young, have sustained feelings for one another over five or six years since first meeting? On Yvonne's side, certainly, this seems improbable. She evidently dated other men during those difficult years and may have thought little about Albert. He was one of many wounded British servicemen she met during the war. With a broken engagement already behind him, by 1922 Albert had asked Patricia to marry him, so it is very unlikely he was still in contact with Yvonne. His

20. ENCOUNTER

fiancé would not tolerate him corresponding with another girl. Nonetheless, did Albert secretly dream of the sweet French girl who had comforted him when he lay wounded in hospital? For many ex-soldiers, waking in a hospital bed to the sight of a pretty girl was a balm so wondrous after the hell of the trenches, they never forgot her face, romanticising about their wartime angel for years after. There were examples of men who *did* go back to France after the war to search for a girl they had fallen for in those dark times. Usually, however, they were relationships that formed in local villages behind the lines where the men were billeted.

Albert, still struggling to adjust to civilian life at this time, was perhaps having second thoughts about marrying Patricia. The sweethearts of returning servicemen found them greatly changed by their experiences and unwittingly said or did the wrong thing, triggering an angry or emotional response. Wives and girlfriends wanted to understand what their men had been through and wanted to help them recover. However many ex-servicemen dreaded being asked 'What was it like?', finding it impossible to answer truthfully, knowing only those who had shared the experience could ever comprehend.

How could any man begin to explain to his girl back home that they had lived like animals in the trenches, their humanity submerged under bestial survival instincts, their thoughts reduced to 'kill or be killed'? Or that the sight of bloody body parts mangled in the mud and the sickly stench of rotting, maggot-infested flesh became so normal it no longer shocked? Anyone who had not been there would recoil in horror if they described what it was really like. It was too awful to remember, let alone share. It was easier, safer, to stay silent.

Well-meaning sympathy from people who couldn't possibly understand was difficult to take, irritating even. In these circumstances, an engagement to be married might easily break, the strain on the relationship too much. Although the Bagley family believe Albert was still engaged to Patricia when he met Yvonne, his departure from London suggests the relationship was faltering. Perhaps Albert felt drawn back to the Somme to search for *his* war-time angel. She had lived in a military zone, helped in the military hospitals and had seen for herself some of the horror. She would understand, without the need for questions and answers.

Whatever Albert's motives were or how he found Yvonne in 1922, they no doubt met in the Abbeville area, where Yvonne continued to live and work after she left state care. At some point after leaving the Metropolitan Police in January of that year, Albert left London bound for France. Travelling from the capital by train to catch a cross-Channel ferry was straightforward.

Among other passengers making the same journey in the early 1920s were numerous grieving widows and parents, on their way to visit the grave of a fallen husband or son. Many families found it very difficult to accept that the body of their loved one, who had died for their country on foreign soil, was not brought home. They could not regularly visit the grave of their loved one to place flowers. Thanks to the work of the IWGC (Imperial War Graves Commission, now called the Commonwealth War Graves Commission), the graveyards they visited were immaculately presented and cared for, as they still are today, and this was some comfort.

The IWGC employed many British ex-servicemen to tend the graveyards. These workers often built a life there, marrying a French woman, sometimes a girl they had met in the war. However, generally it was rare for a former soldier to return. Many never again set foot in northern France: the thought of returning was just too unbearable. But if Albert did not return with the deliberate intention of looking for Yvonne, why did he go there instead of finding work in London? There is no clear answer to this question. Certainly, jobs were hard to come by in Britain at this time. A possible clue lies with one of the witnesses at Albert and Yvonne's wedding the following year, a British man called Thomas Roper. In 1922 Thomas was in France working as an engineer and living at 18 chausée d'Hocquet, not far from the port in Abbeville.

Thomas Roper was likely a friend from Albert's army days. More than one Thomas Roper appears in lists for the London Regiment, although not among surviving records for the 20th Battalion. It was common for regimental pals to stay in touch after the war. Writing to him after the war, Albert maybe confided in Thomas that life in London was not working out well and he needed work. Maybe Thomas encouraged him to come, knowing there were opportunities in Abbeville for English speakers. If Patricia still wore the engagement ring Albert had given her when he sailed for France, she doubtless expected him to return after a few months at most.

Whatever led up to Albert's return to France, he and Thomas were not the only British people in and around Abbeville in the early 1920s. A young English woman who lived near Yvonne, at 30 rue Millevoye, advertised in *Le Pilote de la Somme* around that time, offering English lessons. The British sought each other out, socialising in the same cafés and bars in the town. Among this crowd was another British man, by the name of

20. ENCOUNTER

Denis MacGuire or Guire, possibly also an ex-army friend of Thomas and Albert.[22]

Rue du Maréchal-Foch, Abbeville around 1910. Number 31 was on the right in this photo

The 1921 census shows Denis, just a few years older than Albert, lived at 31 rue du Maréchal Foch with an *amie* (friend) called Marie Rémy and a young *bonne* called Paule Dounette. A 1923 business directory lists Denis as the manager of a dress shop there; clearly he lived above the shop.[23] Rue du Maréchal Foch is one of the main commercial streets in Abbeville. The street had been renamed after the First World War in honour of the French general who commanded the Allied forces in 1918. By the time of Yvonne's marriage in 1923, she was also living at 31 rue du Maréchal Foch. Evidently, after working a short time for the retired couple in rue Millevoye, her last placement as an *enfant de l'Assistance*, she had taken a position working for Denis MacGuire. His dress shop at 31 rue Maréchal Foch was just around the corner, one of several on the street, judging by advertisements in the local papers of the day. Among them were 'Aux Occasions' at number 39 and 'Au Chic Parisien' at number 61. Yvonne had another live-in position, replacing Paule Dounette, after she moved on. Perhaps she hoped, in time, to be asked to serve in the shop or help

22 If Denis MacGuire served with the 20th Londons, his service record appears not to have survived.

23 By the time of the 1926 census the shop was under new management, with a Madame Sophie Mangé and her son living at the address.

alter dresses. However, in the event she did not stay long enough to find out. Her marriage certificate states she was '*sans profession*', implying she was still employed on a casual basis at that point.

Denis MacGuire might be the link who brought Yvonne and Albert together. It is impossible to know the exact circumstances. Perhaps Albert called at the shop to see Denis one day and there was Yvonne. And so Yvonne and Albert's sixty-year relationship began. Their courtship was short, beginning at the earliest in the spring of 1922, depending on when Albert arrived in France. After an extremely cold winter, the weather turned unseasonably warm. Feeling carefree away from London and Patricia, 24-year-old Albert flirted with 21-year-old Yvonne, never imagining his fiancé would find out. The scenes of their courtship were played out in and around Abbeville and may have looked something like this.

> *It is a public holiday. Yvonne and Albert catch a train from Abbeville out to the bay of the Somme. They stroll along the promenade among the crowds at Saint-Valery-sur-Somme to the beacon, just as Yvonne had done on rare occasions with her foster family as a child. Walking back, they hear the tide turn suddenly. From the safety of the promenade, they watch it race up the sand, faster than anyone can run, before flooding to fill the river canal leading eventually to the port at Abbeville. They are charmed to spy a seal bobbing its head above the water as it rides the powerful wave upstream.*
>
> *The pavement terrace of a café. Yvonne and Albert eat moules frites (mussels and chips) at Le Crotoy, the small fishing village across the bay from Saint-Valery, watching the boats come into port. Later they join friends, Denis, Thomas and their sweethearts, on the beach. They remove shoes and stockings to paddle in the shallows, and the girls shriek as the boys jokingly splash them.*
>
> *A Sunday afternoon. Yvonne and Albert stroll together away from the town, along the levelled banks of the Somme river canal. They talk happily in the sunshine, both amused by Albert's faltering French. As the heat rises, they look for a secluded spot where they can be completely alone. The cool shade of the old willow trees provides the perfect place, veiled behind a profusion of wispy branches hanging down like verdant curtains to the water's edge.*

In the sultry days of summer, romance came easily. It would take time, longer than most couples, for Yvonne and Albert to really get to know one another. When Albert first returned to the Somme, his French was inevitably rusty. The necessities of work and daily life helped revive it, but even so, it is unlikely he was sufficiently fluent for deep conversations

20. ENCOUNTER

with Yvonne, and she spoke no English. The language barrier kept their burgeoning relationship simple and light. Both Albert and Yvonne had painful experiences in their past they did not want to talk about.

Yvonne, instinctively ashamed of her background, explained little about her disadvantaged start in life and the turmoil of the past six years. Unlike the Frenchmen she had dated, Albert accepted her as she was and was blind to any stigma of her social status. This was a breath of fresh air for Yvonne, who was used to other people making her feel different and inferior. The cumulative effects of abandonment, loneliness, fear and mistreatment had inevitably taken their toll on her developing character. Albert had no inkling of the harm Yvonne had suffered and the long shadows this would cast over her life.

In the absence of anyone she could confide in, especially after Valentine's death, Yvonne had learnt to suppress the hurt and anger within her. There was no one to reassure her that none of it – abandonment, growing up in care, being mistreated – was her fault. The idea that you could have such conversations was almost unheard of a hundred years ago, in any case. People masked their pain with silence. It is in this silence that dark secrets take root and creep unseen into relationships, creating inexplicable tensions and behaviour.

Yvonne's experiences could have broken her spirit, but instead she reacted by becoming stronger-willed. She fought back against her circumstances, determined to exert some control over her life. Increasingly she pushed the boundaries of her constrained existence to live life her way. If she wanted to go out dancing all night, then she would, although by her early 20s she was more mindful of the consequences and tempered her behaviour.

Outwardly, Yvonne appeared feisty and fun-loving, and these are the qualities Albert first saw in her. If he looked carefully when he gazed into her eyes, he might have glimpsed the vulnerability and slight wariness that lay behind first appearances. Yvonne, in return, did not ask too many questions of Albert, who clearly did not mention Patricia.

As the summer of 1922 turned into autumn, Albert and Yvonne met regularly whenever they had time off from work. At the cinema in town they could watch the latest releases from the once-again-thriving French film industry. They missed some of the on-screen action as they cuddled in the dark. At other times they drank wine together in one of Abbeville's many bars, Albert entertaining Yvonne as he tried in French to describe England, a country that lay not far away over the water but for Yvonne seemed like another world. Little did she imagine in those early days that she would come to spend most of her life there.

Patricia was drifting further and further from Albert's thoughts. Christmas 1922 came and went. Albert continued working in France and seeing Yvonne. It was around this time, in late December 1922 or early January 1923, Yvonne realised she was pregnant. It was no doubt a shock to them both. Albert quickly decided he must do the honourable thing and marry Yvonne, to his credit and her enormous relief. Given the pregnancy, they wanted the wedding to take place as soon as possible.

First Albert had the tricky business of explaining the situation to his parents, Mary and John. They were stunned to learn Albert was breaking off his engagement to marry a French woman he had only recently met. How much he told them isn't known. He possibly failed to mention a baby was already on the way, hoping to explain away the baby's birth as unexpectedly early. Naturally, Patricia was devastated when she found out.

Wedding plans were hastily made.

21: A Quiet Wedding

THE SKY WAS already darkening outside when Yvonne and Albert exchanged their wedding vows at 5.30 pm on Saturday 10 February 1923. They married in a civil ceremony at Abbeville's Hôtel de Ville (town hall). A civil ceremony was essential for their marriage to be legally recognised. Couples who could afford it might also opt for a church ceremony afterwards. This was out of the question for Yvonne and Albert for reasons of cost and the pregnancy.

Hôtel de Ville, Abbeville, pre-1914 (building with grand archway, centre of photo)

The Hôtel de Ville was a large, three-storey, 19th century stone building in the administrative heart of town, on rue de l'Hôtel de Ville. It had a grand archway entrance with huge doors, designed to admit a coach and horses, opening into an interior cobbled courtyard. The building can be seen in photographs and paintings from the 19th and early 20th centuries but has long since disappeared. Along with almost every other building on the street, having survived the bombings of the First World War, it was completely destroyed by the Luftwaffe on 20 May 1940. The ancient belfry that adjoined the Hôtel de Ville was miraculously spared and is all that remains apart from the distinctive curve of the road, which today is a quiet side street known as rue Gontier Patin. After the bombings of the Second World War, the administrative centre of town shifted a short distance into a modern new square, built in the 1950s to cover the huge scar left by the German bombs.

The wedding was a quiet affair, almost certainly with just the bride and groom and the required two witnesses. These were Albert's army friend, Thomas Roper, and another Abbeville resident, Eugène Douzenel, a tailor, whose shop was just along the street from the wedding venue at 27 rue de l'Hôtel de Ville. Eugène perhaps fitted Albert for his wedding suit and was a spontaneous choice of witness. Collecting the suit, Albert asked Eugène if he was free after the shop closed on Saturday as he needed another witness.

There was no announcement of the nuptials in the bi-weekly local paper, *Le Pilote de la Somme*. Interestingly, the week-day edition of the paper before the Saturday of the wedding featured a picture of Tutankhamun's golden death mask on the front page, with a caption about the discovery of his tomb by the English explorer Lord Carnarvon. (The tomb was discovered in November 1922, but the news took time to filter through.)

Yvonne's wedding outfit may have come from the dress shop where she worked at 31 rue du Maréchal Foch, Denis allowing her a discount. Or maybe she sewed it herself. She had to choose carefully. The mid-length, drop-waisted dresses that were in vogue for 1920s brides best suited the tall and willowy, not a short and curvy woman expecting a baby, although her youth and the loose fit were on her side.

There are no known photos of the big day but Albert and Yvonne made a distinctive couple. Albert 5 foot 9 and three-quarter inches tall, and thin with an upright military bearing, his bride beside him not much taller than 5 feet even in heels. Although Yvonne had long dark hair when Albert met her, she maybe had it cut fashionably short for the occasion. She certainly wore it this way for the rest of her life.

At the end of a short ceremony, the couple sat at a desk opposite the marriage official, Charles Boujonnier, as he reached for his nib pen, dipped it in a pot of ink and asked Yvonne and Albert for the details required for the *Actes de Marriages* (marriage register). Theirs was the twenty-second marriage to take place at Abbeville's Hôtel de Ville in 1923. After the official had completed the long, wordy entry, the newlyweds and their two witnesses took it in turns to borrow his pen and sign at the bottom of the

21: A QUIET WEDDING

register entry. Albert signed first, his writing small, neat and on a slant. Yvonne went next and she followed Albert's lead exactly, signing her name directly under his, almost a mirror image, on the same slant, in handwriting every bit as tidy. She was unused to signing important documents. Feeling unsure and wanting to get it right, she took her cue from Albert. After the two witnesses had signed, their handwriting less constrained, the official added his own signature, with a final flourish of his pen.

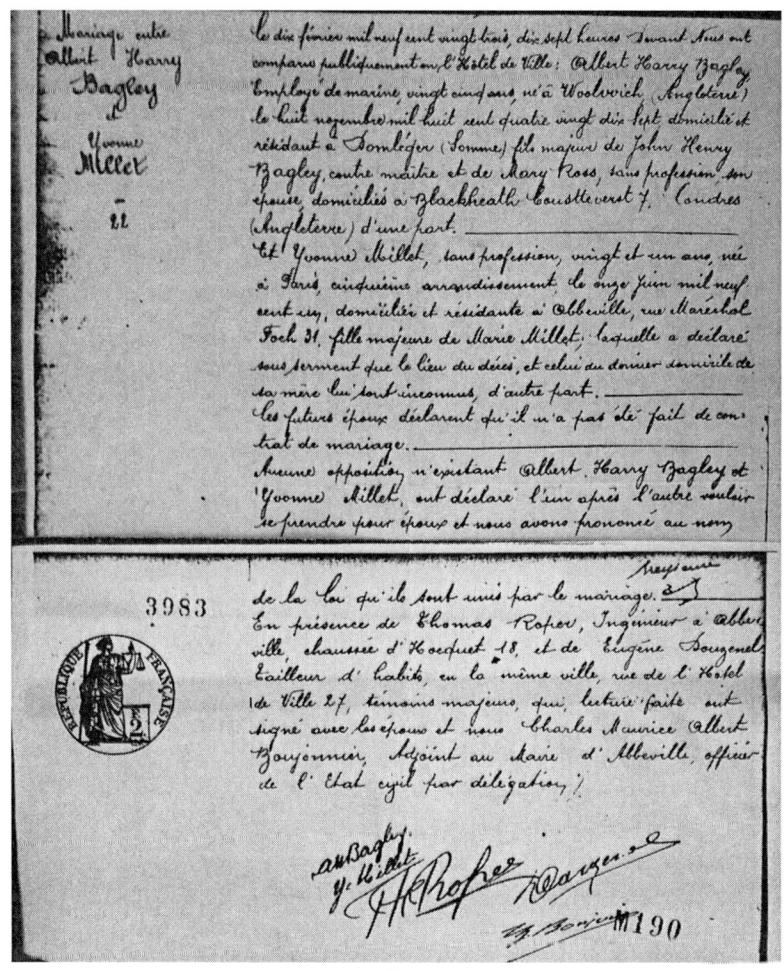

Register entry for Yvonne and Albert's marriage in February 1923

As they left the Hôtel de Ville at around 6 pm, Yvonne wore a coat or stole around her shoulders for warmth in the evening chill and a cloche hat, pulled low to shade eyes that shone with excitement and relief. Yvonne was already two months pregnant.

Albert did not walk away from his responsibilities to his unborn child, even though it meant hurting Patricia. Everything happened so fast that Albert and Yvonne may never have paused to consider if they were truly in love. Albert was from a respectable family and he understood what was required of him in the circumstances. Love did not necessarily come into it. Yet his decision to marry Yvonne saved her, and their child, from untold misery. Her father's failure to stand by her mother had a profound effect on both their lives. Marriage spared Yvonne from the poverty trap that had engulfed her mother. Even in 1923, as a single mother with no home of her own, qualified only for poorly paid casual work as a *bonne*, circumstances could easily have forced Yvonne to give up her baby to state care.

Yvonne and Albert were a young bride and groom, but not uncommonly so: Yvonne was 21 and Albert 25 years old. The moment when they placed gold bands on one another's fingers was a turning point for Yvonne, without doubt the best thing that could have happened to her given her background and the era in which she lived. It changed the course of her life immeasurably for the better, although she may not have always appreciated this. Not only did she marry, but her husband was a good man from a respectable lower middle-class English family, her father-in-law employed in a first-rung managerial position as a foreman – '*contremaître*' – according to the marriage record. In the group portrait of 1915 the Bagley family are all well-dressed and Albert's father John is wearing a smart pocket watch across his waistcoat. The match Yvonne had made would have impressed anyone who knew her.

Yvonne's happiness that day was tinged with sadness at Valentine's absence. It is possible Yvonne told Alfred Desjardins she was getting married, although there is no evidence he went along to wish the newlyweds well. He was moving on with his life after losing Valentine two years previously. Alfred was soon to marry again, on 26 May 1923. He was 51 years old and his new wife, Amélia Marie Blond, was 29.

By the time of the 1926 census in Allery, Alfred and Amélia, known by her family as Lydia, had a two-year-old daughter, Héloise Alfreda. Later the same year, on 17 June 1926, their son Gaston was born. Alfred and Lydia lived on rue du Bout de la Ville, Allery on the other side of the village from the home Alfred had shared with Valentine and their foster children. Having survived the war, and after the sorrow of losing Valentine, he had made a fresh start and was raising a family of his own.

Sadly, his newfound happiness was short-lived. Alfred was by now working as a tradesman specialising in zinc roofs. On 27 June 1926, just ten days after Gaston's birth, tragedy struck. Alfred fell from a roof he was

21: A QUIET WEDDING

working on and was killed. He is buried in the cemetery at Allery. His name lives on through four more generations of the Desjardins family. His daughter Héloise had two children and his son Gaston had eight. Alfred's grandchildren produced thirteen children between them and six grandchildren to date. Some still live in Allery today, including his granddaughter Maryline (born 1963).

It is also doubtful that Yvonne's younger foster sister Marguerite Bourdon, by now aged seventeen, attended the wedding. There was a five-year age gap between them and it seems unlikely they stayed in touch, especially if they did not get on well. After Marguerite left Valentine and Alfred's care, she stayed in Allery and appears in the 1921 census working as a *bonne* in the village. She had left Allery by the time of the census in 1926, the year she turned twenty-one, and no doubt moved around placements several times over the years, just as Yvonne had done.

There is no surviving evidence of where Yvonne and Albert lived initially as newlyweds. Perhaps Yvonne moved in with Albert at first. The marriage record states Albert was living at Domléger, a small commune 20 kilometres north-east of Abbeville. There is no street name or house number on the record, so it is impossible to know exactly where he lived. (He was not in Domléger at the time of a census.)

The marriage record also states Albert was working as a merchant seaman ('*employé de marine*'). Who employed him remains a mystery and it was possibly only casual work, because a short while later he took another job. Albert might have been based at the port of Abbeville. This was still operating in 1923 and maybe there was work for an Englishman who spoke some French.

There was a long history of trade through the port because of its easy access to the sea along the River Somme. By 1923 the port was in serious decline although vessels still docked with coal, fertilisers, sugar beet and other goods for local industries. There was a sugar plant in the town until 2007 (the chimney remains as a monument on the redeveloped site), plus breweries, a distillery and mills. Rope, carpets and textiles, in particular linens and tablecloths, were made in the town. Perhaps Albert was involved in the export of textiles, which would later lead him to work in the textile industry in Lille.

If Albert was working out of the port in Abbeville, it is strange that he was living in Domléger. It was not a convenient location. Lodgings were readily available in a town the size of Abbeville but from Domléger, the port was a 20 kilometre cycle or bus ride away.

Another interesting revelation on the marriage record is that by then,

Yvonne knew more about her origins. She stated correctly her place of birth was the 5th arrondissement in Paris and her mother's name was Marie Millet. Yvonne had only recently acquired this information. Growing up, she knew nothing about her mother or the circumstances of her birth.

Naturally, many *enfants de l'Assistance* yearned to trace their mother. Girls usually waited until they turned 21, knowing the law decreed the information would be withheld until they left state care so there was little point in trying. Boys tended to make enquiries earlier. During military service, they would see other lads opening letters from home, and felt acutely the absence of any mail addressed to them. This spurred them to seek answers, but to no avail. Even into the 21st century, France remains one of the most difficult countries for fostered and adopted children to get information about their biological families.

When Marie vanished completely from Yvonne's life, Yvonne was too young to retain memories of her, or of her infrequent visits to Thiepval. Flickers of memory conflated with vague memories of Victorine Talon, the first true mother figure in her life. Yvonne was only three and a half when taken into state care. From that time on, her mother's identity was kept secret. Her forthcoming wedding prompted Yvonne to ask Assistance Publique for information.

Under oath, Yvonne told the marriage official her mother was deceased, her last address unknown. Yet there is no evidence Yvonne knew for certain Marie was dead. There is nothing on her Assistance Publique file to confirm Marie's fate. The authorities had little interest in what happened to Marie. In their view, an abandoned child should not be reunited with their biological families unless stringent conditions were met, because they had failed in the task of parenting. The state took over the responsibility for raising these children with the goal of turning them into law-abiding, self-sufficient adults who contributed to the economy and would not be a drain on public finances. Preferably they would remain in the French countryside, where they were most needed. In Yvonne's case, with her marriage, the state had fulfilled its purpose to a very satisfactory degree, despite some bumps along the way.

There are a number of possible reasons why Yvonne claimed her mother was dead. Firstly, she may have felt too ashamed to tell Albert she had been abandoned by her mother when, inevitably, he asked about her family. It was easier to say her mother was dead and, of course, the woman she regarded as her mother, Valentine, had died. We can only speculate whether or when and how Yvonne introduced Albert to Alfred. Inevitably, over the years, Albert would come to understand the truth. But he never

21: A QUIET WEDDING

knew the complete story of his wife's start in life, because Yvonne's earliest years were a mystery even to her. It is doubtful that Assistance Publique allowed Yvonne to read her own file, instead sharing only the basic facts of her place of birth, mother's name and the date she was taken into care.

Secondly, Yvonne may have grown up believing her mother had died. Perhaps the Desjardins allowed her to believe this, to spare her the pain of knowing she had been abandoned. However, it seems unlikely Yvonne would have reached the age of 21 without suspecting her mother had not died but had abandoned her. She knew most *enfants de l'Assistance* were abandoned children. Playground chatter alone was enough for her to question whether she was really an orphan.

The third possibility is that Assistance Publique did confirm to Yvonne that Marie was no longer alive. In early 1905, when the authorities tried to trace Marie, they might have discovered she had died. If there was originally a note to this effect on Yvonne's file, a loose piece of paper along with others in the slim buff coloured folder, it was somehow lost over the decades. But this is an unlikely scenario. If Marie had died, it was not in Paris. There is no record of her death in the city registers around the time Yvonne was abandoned.

If Marie was still alive, she was around 50 years old in 1923 when Yvonne and Albert married. If she was still in domestic service, she would have been increasingly fearful of losing her position. Finding new employment was very difficult for older *domestiques*, who aged prematurely, their health and strength declining after decades of hard physical toil. Households wanted young, robust girls they could work hard. Unemployment at this stage of her life could be catastrophic. Unless she had savings and was extremely resourceful, her only option would be to enter a hospice, with little prospect of ever leaving again. Life for older inhabitants of the hospice was bleak. Men and women were segregated. There was little to fill the endless hours beside a stroll around the courtyard and the company of other unfortunates, who shared frugal meals in the refectory and slept in cheerless dormitories. Bedtime was at sunset even in winter, to save on energy bills.

On the other hand, over the years Marie's luck may have changed. Perhaps she had found happiness with a good man who gave her security, more children and a proper family life. There is no way of knowing and Marie's fate remains a mystery.

Whatever really happened to Marie after January 1905, Yvonne spent her entire childhood not knowing where she had come from or even who her mother was. Discovering at the age of 21 her place of birth and her mother's name was cold comfort. Nothing could change the past or shake off the legacy of being an *enfant de l'Assistance*. Whether she realised it or not, she was blessed to have met Albert, a patient, strong, reliable man. Their marriage was the start of a secure future for her.

Sometime in the weeks or months immediately after the wedding, Albert and Yvonne left Abbeville. There was no question of starting married life in London; Albert would rather family, friends and especially Patricia did not find out the real reason for his hasty marriage. He wanted to protect the family reputation. Albert needed a permanent job in France that paid enough to support his new family. Moving away from Abbeville also avoided curiosity about the conception out of wedlock, although there was less stigma attached to this in France.

Albert found a job with F. N. Pickett et Fils, a company contracted to clear and defuse ammunition left all over the conflict zone after the war. The company processed and sold the metals and other materials recovered, supplying hungry industries in the post-war period of rebuilding. Established by a young British entrepreneur with an electrical engineering background, it was a highly successful enterprise. The 'et Fils' in the company name was the owner's small son Bobby.

By 1923, F. N. Pickett et Fils had grown into big business. There were ten factories, nine in northern France and the other in Belgium. Two factories were in the Somme, at Saigneville near Saint Valéry-sur-Somme and at Fressenneville. The headquarters was in Wimereux on the northern coast of France, just east of Boulogne-sur-Mer, and it is here that Albert worked in a clerical role. His language skills were an asset to the firm, whose customers included the British and French governments.

Albert and Yvonne found a home at Wimereux, where their first child was born on 6 September 1923. The baby was named Gordon after his uncle, Albert's younger brother. As was not unusual at the time, their exact address is not stated on the birth certificate. It only reveals the district where they lived: Pierre Napoléon, on the outskirts of the town near an important monument of the same name. Pierre Napoléon marks the spot where Napoleon Bonaparte sat, on 16 August 1804, to distribute the cross of the Légion d'Honneur to his army.

At last, Yvonne had a family and a home to call her own. Yet marriage and motherhood were not perhaps the complete joy she imagined. She was only 22 years old and unprepared for having a baby. Her life after leaving state care was only just beginning. Any sense of freedom she had felt was immediately lost to the demands of a newborn and running a home. Pierre Napoléon was a windswept and rather isolated place to live,

21: A QUIET WEDDING

on high ground looking out over the choppy grey waters of the English Channel. The town was a bus ride away down the hill. It was lonely for Yvonne at home all day with the baby while Albert was out at work.

The first known photo of Yvonne was taken around this time. It is a family portrait, no doubt taken in the studio of a local photographer in Wimereux. Yvonne looks vulnerable and wary, in need of mothering herself, as she cradles her baby in her arms. Albert sits to her right. Neither are smiling. Young, inexperienced and tired from broken nights, they have not thought to take the dummy out of baby Gordon's mouth for the photo. It is a poignant image.

Albert, Yvonne and baby Gordon, around late 1923. This is the earliest surviving photo of Yvonne

Part Six: Family Life, 1923 onwards

22: Domesticity

DESPITE THE ADVERSITY of the first twenty-one years of her life, after her marriage to Albert, Yvonne was never again alone in the world. Up to that point, she had suffered so much loneliness and loss. By the age of three she had been cut permanently adrift from her blood relatives and by the age of nineteen she had lost her dear foster mother, Valentine. Yvonne filled the void in her heart, consciously or otherwise, by creating her own large family with her husband. At last, she had people to whom she belonged.

The couple eventually had seven children. The teachings of the Catholic church, instilled in Yvonne during her childhood, may have had something to do with the size of their family. However, large families were also widely admired in France for other reasons. Having lots of children was actively encouraged as part of the drive to replenish the population and, after the First World War, this was more important than ever. Two national awards were created in the early 1920s to honour parents who raised several children, the Prix Cognacq-Jay and the Médaille de la Famille française. The arrival of Yvonne and Albert's fifth child could have led to a cash prize under the Cognacq-Jay scheme and when their sixth child was born, they qualified for the Silver Médaille. But there is no evidence they applied for either accolade.

All the Bagley children were given English first names. Presumably, Albert had the final say on that. Deep down, at some level, perhaps he knew they would one day settle in England, where it would be easier for their children to have English names. Yvonne of course had no family names to pass on beside her own, and no inclination to pass on the name of the mother who abandoned her. To the children, Yvonne and Albert were the English 'Mum' and 'Dad'.

Their second child, Ian, arrived in January 1925, a younger brother for Gordon. In 1928, the year Yvonne turned 27 years old, the couple's third son, Archibald Bruce, was born. Archie, as he was known, was named after a Bagley ancestor who was head gamekeeper at a Scottish castle in the 19th century.

22: DOMESTICITY

By now the family were living in Roubaix, a town in the metropolitan area of Lille, close to the border with Belgium. Albert had left F.N. Pickett et Fils and taken a new job with La Lainière, one of several woollen mills in the Lille area. With a growing family, he was attracted by better wages. Roubaix had a long history of cloth manufacturing, specialising in wool. La Lainière was established in 1911, at a time of prosperity in Roubaix, which came to an abrupt halt in the First World War, when the Germans looted and destroyed the factory. In the post-war period La Lainière rose again and between 1920 and 1930 became the most important and modern mill in Europe. Albert was one of 8,000 people the company employed on its site at 149, rue d'Oran in Roubaix.

119 rue de l'Ouest, Roubaix today (right of picture)

The metropolitan area of Lille kept good records. Every year, a directory of citizens and businesses was published by Ravet Anceau, thick volumes with a distinctive red cover. The Ravet Anceau directory covered Lille and Roubaix in detail. Copies for most years still survive in the departmental archives at Lille. Albert Bagley is listed in the 1929 edition living at 119 rue de l'Ouest, Roubaix. There is no record of when the family moved there, although they were not yet at this address when the 1926 census was taken. 119 rue de l'Ouest is in a row of 19th century, three-storey, red-brick terraced houses, still standing today. A widowed pensioner called Madame Dujardin also lived at number 119, indicating the house was divided into apartments, with the Bagley family living in one and Madame

Dujardin in the other. Next door at number 117 lived a painter and on the other side, at number 121 a lithographer. Certainly, rue de l'Ouest was a convenient location, close to the railway station and less than three kilometres from the La Lainière factory. Albert could easily walk or cycle to work each morning.

While Albert sat behind a desk all day, Yvonne's work was physically and emotionally demanding. The hours were entirely taken up with caring for the children, washing, cleaning and cooking. In the late 1920s, running a home still involved hard, physical labour for those who could not afford help. Domestic appliances were starting to become commonplace but their cost put them out of reach for most people. Yvonne still lugged water from a pump and did the laundry with washing dollies and flat irons heated on the range. Without a fridge to preserve food, she shopped daily for groceries, her young children in tow. The household budget was meagre and she had to make it stretch increasingly far as the family grew. It was exhausting and at times she felt overwhelmed. She had no time to call her own.

By 1931, Yvonne and Albert had moved home again, and were listed in the Ravet Anceau directory living at 72 rue Saint Joseph, Roubaix. A photo of Gordon, Ian and Archie was taken in this street around this time. Although not cheap, Albert had bought one of the first cameras that became available by the early 1930s, probably the Kodak Brownie.

On Sundays, the family attended Saint-François Catholic church, a huge place built in the late 1850s standing at the end of rue Saint Joseph. Instinctively, Yvonne was repeating an influential part of her own childhood by raising her children as Catholics. She had comforting memories not only of the life of Sainte-Trinité church, with its familiar rituals and celebrations, but also of the kindly nuns at the hospices in Amiens and Abbeville. The Catholic faith had always offered her a safe embrace of acceptance and belonging and she continued to hold it dear in her adult life.

The family budget also stretched to seaside visits. A photo taken around 1932 shows the Bagley family on holiday at Boulogne-sur-Mer, near their former home in Wimereux. They stand close together to pose for the photographer on a pier, their backs to the sea, with a distinctive-shaped beacon behind them. The pier and beacon still exist. Gordon, the oldest boy, is holding a bucket and spade. There is a look of protest on his face at being made to stand still for the photo when he is itching to get on the beach and make sand castles. Albert holds his youngest child Heather, born in May 1931, in the crook of his left arm. Albert's right hand gently

22: DOMESTICITY

restrains his impatient oldest son by the shoulder. Yvonne looks happy and proud of her young family.

The Bagley family on holiday in Boulogne-sur-Mer c.1932

An individual photo of Archie, aged four and dressed in the same clothes as in the seaside photo, has a note on the back that reads 'rue du Sapin Vert, Tourcoing'. Sometime around 1933, they had moved home again. Tourcoing is another town in the Lille metropolitan area, adjacent to Wattrelos and Roubaix, right on the Belgian border. It was while here that Albert and Yvonne's second daughter Cynthia Joan was born on 1 April 1934, followed two years later by their fourth son, Ronald, born on 7 March 1936. Another family photo dated 1936 shows Gordon, Ian, Archie, Cynthia and Heather on the beach, the sun in their eyes, at Middlekerke,

Belgium. This popular family resort was in easy reach for a family holiday, around 100 kilometres from their home in Tourcoing.

A further house move followed, around 1937, this time back to Roubaix, to the Croix district, where Gordon Bagley recalled there was a large British community. Perhaps this was the attraction of the move, but it may also have been prompted by Gordon's schooling. After the age of eleven, he was enrolled at the Turgot Institute in Roubaix, which specialised in vocational training. It was a long walk from their former home in Wattrelos to the Turgot Institute. Gordon told his son Chris they lived in a large house opposite a sports club, where Albert enjoyed games of rugby (probably as a spectator: he was by now in his mid-30s). The local park was Parc Barbieux, a restful place to wander and for the children to play, with its peaceful waterfalls and rock gardens. A modern new public swimming pool had opened in Roubaix in 1932, designed in a lavish Art Deco style.[24] The Bagley children may have learnt to swim here, encouraged by Albert. As a boy, growing up in London, Albert had been a local swimming club champion. With its well-kept green spaces and modern leisure attractions, Roubaix was a well-chosen place to raise a family.

There is some suggestion (from Chris' conversations with his father) that they moved yet again, back to the area near Saint-François church in Roubaix, to a large apartment. Gordon remembered that the family still continued to go to church in Croix on Sundays, and this was almost certainly Saint-Martin's Catholic church. Being part of a church congregation was important for Yvonne in more ways than one. It gave her social contact she otherwise lacked.

Over the ten years to 1934, the family moved house at least five times, living in three different towns (Wimereux, Roubaix and Wattrelos). The disruption was particularly hard for Yvonne who was largely isolated at home from Monday to Friday, with the demands of family life increasing as the family grew. It was difficult for her to get to know anyone in her neighbourhood, especially as they did not stay anywhere very long.

Looking after children alone all day is of course exhausting and a test of any parent's resolve, especially with so many little ones wanting attention. They did not start school until they turned six years of age. Yvonne loved babies but could readily lose patience with the older children. She had no extended family to call on for help and no mother to ask for advice. Parentless her whole life, parenthood did not come easily. And she was

---

24 Today it is an art gallery called La Piscine. It retains many of the original Art Deco features.

22: DOMESTICITY

still in domestic servitude of a kind. Even though she was mistress in her own home, and working for her husband and children rather than strangers, the exhausting daily round of chores were just the same. She certainly had plenty of experience to deal with the practicalities of running the home and her son Ron remembers she was a very good cook. In this respect she took after her mother, Marie. Her sewing skills were not put to use: she had no time.

23: Leaving France

UNFORTUNATELY, THE GOOD times in Lille's textile industry did not last. The world slump of the 1930s led to bitter strikes as owners sought to cut wages and impose less favourable working conditions. Change was in the air. More troubling than this were the terrible events unfolding in Germany, under Hitler's Nazi regime. By late 1938 another war seemed inevitable. This prospect, coupled with job uncertainty, forced Albert and Yvonne to consider their situation. If they stayed in France, Albert was warned, he could be called up for French military service. Worse still, the threat of a German invasion was very real.

Albert began making plans to take Yvonne and the children to England, seeking help from his family there. With six children to feed and clothe, his wages as a clerk left little to spare. Somehow, he scraped together the means to relocate the family across the Channel, but when they first arrived, probably in late 1938, they had nowhere to live. Gordon, the eldest, was by now aged sixteen and the youngest, Ron, just three. The family was forced to split up and lodge with two or three different Bagley relatives in the Sussex area until accommodation for them all could be found.

Eventually, Albert's youngest sister Catherine came to the rescue. She worked for the local council in Welwyn Garden City, Hertfordshire and helped the family get a council house in the town. Sometime before late September 1939, they moved into their new home at 18 Athelstan Walk. The British government conducted a special wartime census, the 1939 Register, on the night of 29 September, just weeks after the outbreak of war. The family are listed on the register at this address and they were settled enough that Albert had already found a job. Yvonne and Albert would make 18 Athelstan Walk their home for over 45 years.

Athelstan Walk was a cul-de-sac of twenty-six homes, one of a cluster of five similar streets off the main Broadwater Road. The estate sat on a wedge of land between the main road, the railway line to London and the town's industrial area. This was not the most desirable part of town,

23: LEAVING FRANCE

but the white-painted houses were thoughtfully designed and their large windows let in plenty of light.

Number 18 was about halfway down on the right-hand side of Athelstan Walk, a small terraced house with a long garden backing onto the grounds of a factory, Roche Products Ltd. It had the modern comfort of an indoor bathroom, most likely a first for Yvonne and Albert, but with only two bedrooms it was cramped for a large, boisterous family.

Leaving France was difficult for Yvonne, and she was doubtless very upset at the turn of events. Germany, the hated enemy, was threatening her country yet again, this time driving her from home and disrupting the life she and Albert had built. Much of her life to this point had been characterised by unwelcome changes forced on her by circumstance, and in many ways she was well-adapted to cope. This time, however, it was different and it is understandable if she was nervous about what lay ahead. She had never been to England before, had not met her in-laws and did not speak the language. Although Yvonne was reluctant to go, the family had a lucky escape.

❖ ❖ ❖ ❖ ❖

Less than a year later, in May 1940, the Nazis swept through Belgium into France. Beaten into retreat, Allied troops became trapped on the beaches of Dunkirk and a huge rescue operation was mounted from Dover on the English coast. It was quickly realised the British Navy did not have available capacity to avert mass slaughter of the trapped men. The Government called on the nation's boat owners to help.

Between 26 May and 4 June, 300,000 troops were evacuated from the beaches, many borne away to safety aboard a flotilla of small craft piloted by brave civilians, who answered the call. Aboard some boats were French children whose parents had rushed them to the beaches to try and get them away to safety. They were not turned away. Soldiers shielded the terrified youngsters from the bullets as the boats made the agonising journey to the other side of the Channel. Despite the success of this extraordinary and now legendary operation, thousands of soldiers were taken prisoner by the Germans or perished under enemy fire before they could be saved.

As the Germans swept south towards Paris and westwards towards the Somme, tens of thousands of civilians began to flee, many on foot. In Allery, Louis Allot's wife left with their two daughters in the early hours of Saturday 19 May, to seek shelter with friends in Rennes. Louis stayed behind.

Had the Bagley family stayed in the Lille region, one of the first areas to come under German occupation, they would have faced real peril. From July 1940, the Nazis began a round-up of three thousand British nationals in occupied France. The ordeal would begin with an ominous knock on the door, often in the early hours of the morning. The German soldiers came for the men and older boys first, allowing them five minutes to pack a small case. They did not say where they would be going or for how long.

Initially, the British captives were taken to temporary centres before eventually winding up in detention camps in Germany. Many of the men seized in the Lille area were transported to a camp at Tost, more than 1,000 kilometres away near the Polish border. The transfer out east typically lasted more than three days, travelling by rail in cattle trucks, often without food or water. On arrival, the exhausted men discovered the camp offered little comfort beyond whatever possessions they had hastily packed when arrested. The Nazis paid no regard to the Geneva Convention of 1929, even though Germany was a signatory. Detainees slept on the hard floor and at times resorted to eating grass and scavenged potato peelings in a desperate attempt to stave off hunger. As days turned into weeks, then months and years, the arrival of Red Cross parcels and a trickle of communication with loved ones alleviated some of their suffering. Nonetheless, several British men died in the camps through illness or suicide.

In most cases, soon after the men had been taken away, their French wives and children were also rounded up and interned in camps in Nazi-occupied France. Those who survived the ordeal waited five long years to be reunited with their family, after the camps were liberated by US troops in April 1945.

❖ ❖ ❖ ❖ ❖

Safely in England, Yvonne assumed their stay would be temporary, just until the war was over.

Disorientated in an unfamiliar land, she sought out the constancy of the Catholic church and the family resumed their routine of going to Sunday morning services. They attended St Bonaventure's, a twenty-minute walk from home, the town's first and, until the early 1960s, only Catholic church. It was attached to a small convent, established in 1922 by three adventurous Sisters of the Canossian Daughters of Charity, from Milan,

23: LEAVING FRANCE

Italy. The occasional sight of the serene nuns gave Yvonne a reassuring sense of familiarity. It is a shame for her they were not French.

Even though the family successfully created a new life in England, Yvonne never gave up hope they would one day return to France. Other French wives of First World War veterans living in Britain also yearned to go home and many succeeded in persuading their husbands. Yvonne was not one of them. Her husband knew there was too much to give up in England.

Albert, aged 41 at the outbreak of the Second World War, was thankfully too old for active service in the British army. He found work as a senior general clerk with Murphy Radio, at their factory a short distance from Athelstan Walk, along Broadwater Road. During the war, business was good for Murphy Radio, which switched to making radio sets for use by the British Armed Forces. Opposite Murphy Radio stood the huge Shredded Wheat factory, which produced breakfast cereals on the site until 2008. Yvonne's grandson, Chris Bagley, recalls the smell of breakfast cereal drifting on the breeze.

St Bonaventure's Church, Welwyn Garden City, today

Later on, Albert took a job in the statistical division at ICI Plastics, on the outskirts of the town, around half an hour's walk from home. This was possibly still during the war, when the demand for plastics grew significantly. Perspex was needed for the enclosed cockpits and shaped canopies of Royal Air Force fighter planes. Secure employment, a home and, for Albert at least, the proximity of his relatives, anchored the family in England long-term. They settled permanently in Welwyn Garden City and although Yvonne may not have wanted to be there, it was a good place to put down roots.

Welwyn Garden City has changed little over the decades and is a protected conservation area. Today, it remains a desirable place to live, with its well-laid out, low-rise town centre, generous tree-lined boulevards and green open spaces. Although called a 'city' it is a modest-sized town, founded by the social reformer Sir Ebenezer Howard. He had a vision of healthy towns combining the best of city and countryside, created from scratch on greenfield sites. The first town created to his 'garden city' model was Letchworth, where building started in 1906. Work on Welwyn Garden City, the second and often considered the finest of its kind, began in 1920. Eventually, Howard's much-admired model inspired similar projects the world over, including as far afield as Canberra, Australia. When Yvonne and Albert arrived in the late 1930s, Welwyn Garden City was in its infancy and their house little more than ten years old.

◆ ◆ ◆ ◆ ◆

The war cast its shadow over the family's early years in Welwyn Garden City.

In July 1940, Yvonne and Albert's oldest son Gordon enlisted in the British army. Like his father before him, he lied about his age to join up, claiming to have been born in September 1921. In reality, he was only 16 years old. Albert could hardly object even if he did not approve.

In this war, Albert 'dug for victory' instead of digging trenches, growing vegetables to feed the family. Rationing and queuing added to the difficulties of everyday life. There were air raids and nights spent in shelters. Although Welwyn Garden City was not a particular target for the Germans, its situation just north of London put the town at risk. Over 200 homes were damaged by bombs during the course of the war, with two completely destroyed and at least two people killed. Thankfully, Athelstan Walk was spared.

For Yvonne, the war brought back dark memories of fear and bombs in Abbeville and Pont-Rémy more than twenty years previously. This time, she was a refugee from her homeland but she did not have to suffer the war alone: she had family by her side. She was not even the only refugee from mainland Europe in Welwyn Garden City. A group of concerned local people had formed a committee in the 1930s to rescue German Jews from Nazi persecution and give them shelter in the town. A hostel was

23: LEAVING FRANCE

opened for them in Applecroft Road, a mile away from the Bagley family home.

In 1943 the couple's last child, Eric, was born. The birth of this late baby was a bittersweet event. Gordon, aged 19, was serving in Burma at the time. As Yvonne sat by the wireless nursing the new baby, she would hear notes of melancholy in Vera Lynn's voice singing 'We'll meet again', even if she didn't understand all the words. Ian also joined the army and in 1944, when he was 19, was involved in the D-Day landings. Thankfully, both Gordon and Ian eventually returned home safely.

VE Day street party in Athelstan Walk, 9 May 1945
Courtesy of Welwyn Times and Hertfordshire Archives & Local Studies

❖ ❖ ❖ ❖ ❖

After the end of the Second World War, certainly from 1948 onwards, Yvonne and Albert took the younger children to France every August. Ron remembers well the family holidays in Allery, when they visited Yvonne's childhood friend Louis Allot. Yvonne always spoke fondly to her children of Louis and his wife Paule, who they addressed respectfully as 'Madame Allot'. Yvonne and Louis had stayed in touch, despite all the upheavals in

Yvonne's life, their respective marriages and two world wars. Louis and Paule opened their home to the Bagleys for their summer visits.

Yvonne with her daughters Heather (left) and Cynthia (right) in Paris, sometime between the end of the war and May 1953

The Allots lived at La Maison au Soleil on rue de la Liberté and Louis' mother Camille Allot came to live next door. Camille was a formidable woman, according to her grandson Frédéric Defente. She built a house for herself on adjoining land from where, in her later years, she could more easily keep an eye on her only son. Yvonne would have known Camille, who died in 1970, quite well.

Louis and Paule had married in 1928, five years after Yvonne and Albert. 'Madame Allot' was by all accounts a lovely lady, always cheerful and thoughtful, and musically talented. She was a devout Catholic and regularly attended mass at Sainte-Trinité, where she played the organ and harmonium. Louis and Paule's two daughters, Bernadette and Jaqueline, known affectionately as Nadette and Jacotte, were playmates for the Bagley children when they visited.

La Maison au Soleil wasn't big enough to accommodate all the visiting Bagleys. Ron recalls he and some of his siblings stayed with a couple he knew as 'Oncle Albert' and 'Madame Charlotte', who lived close by. This couple were almost certainly the former close neighbours of the Desjar-

23: LEAVING FRANCE

dins on chemin de Mérélessart: Albert and Charlotte Mullier,[25] parents of Yvonne's childhood friend Jeanne. Yvonne was occasionally heard to speak of 'Madame Charlotte' being 'like a mother to me', suggesting Yvonne had a warm relationship with her when growing up in the close-knit Quayet neighbourhood. She may have especially valued Charlotte's friendship after Valentine died.

The family holidays in Allery are the clearest possible evidence that Yvonne's childhood years there were happy; she returned because of warm memories and good friends. She had regarded Valentine and Alfred as her parents, to the extent she let her own children believe they were her biological parents. Her 'father', she mentioned vaguely, had worked in the metal trade. When Yvonne was fostered by the Desjardins, Alfred worked first as a chimney sweep and later as a roofer working with zinc. Valentine and Alfred having long since died, it wasn't difficult for Yvonne to continue to let her children believe they were her real parents. Albert of course must have known the truth by the time the family regularly visited Allery, where the Desjardins were remembered. Louis Allot and Sosthène Dufour, of course, also knew the reality.

✦ ✦ ✦ ✦ ✦

Life continued in Welwyn Garden City, Albert working to support the family, Yvonne fully occupied with running the home. She would walk with the younger children to meet Albert at the factory gates as he left work every evening. French was the first language spoken at home and all Yvonne and Albert's children grew up bilingual. Yvonne ruled the roost and her children nick-named her 'Napoleon'. Home life was at times far from tranquil and there were fearsome rows. Inevitably, under the strains and stresses of everyday life, Yvonne's bottled-up emotions from past traumas occasionally burst forth. The children were ever wary of Yvonne's volatile temperament and controlling ways.

She rarely mentioned her childhood in France, occasionally alluding to her 'parents' and her 'sister', Marguerite, who she 'did not get on with'. She was also heard to mention a 'brother' who had died in the First World War; however, there is no surviving evidence to indicate who she had in mind. Perhaps he was a boy she had known as a child in the Quayet

---

25 Joseph Albert Mullier was known as Albert or by his nickname Ch'Kroumir. They are remembered in Allery as 'fine people'.

neighbourhood, a few years older than her, whose name is carved in the war memorial outside Allery's mairie.

Yvonne with Archie, 1969

Yvonne and Albert shrouded the date of their wedding anniversary in mystery, and it was never celebrated. They did not want their children to know Yvonne had been pregnant when they married. With the subject of the past closed, the children had no idea of the suffering Yvonne had endured growing up and could not understand what lay behind her unpredictable behaviour and outbursts. With such a large family in a small house, there was little privacy or escape from the tensions. One by one, as soon as they were old enough, each of the children left home, keen to fly the crowded nest and make their own lives.

In May 1953 Yvonne and Albert were dealt a devastating blow when their daughter Heather died in a motorcycle accident at the age of eighteen. This was yet another terrible loss for Yvonne added to the mountain of loss she had accumulated at a young age.

When Yvonne and Albert's second eldest son Ian married a German

23: LEAVING FRANCE

woman, Inge, Yvonne was aghast. As a child of the First World War and a refugee from her homeland in the Second World War, it felt like a betrayal and caused a serious rift in the family.

In time, grandchildren began to arrive, including Jan Bagley, Archie's younger daughter, who was born in October 1960. Growing up in Surrey, Jan remembers regularly hearing her father talking on the phone in French to Yvonne. However, she rarely saw her *Grand-mère* or *Grand-père*, as she called Yvonne and Albert, perhaps just twice a year. Yvonne and Albert never owned a car and their house was too small for Jan and her family to stay overnight. The journey across London to visit Welwyn Garden City, though only about 60 miles, was not an easy one. However, vivid memories stick in Jan's mind of childhood visits to 18 Athelstan Walk. She recalls:

> 'I can picture the Athelstan Walk house very clearly. I really liked the house, a simple 2 up, 2 down layout. It was white and clean looking on the outside, sharp and graphically strong, modern. Downstairs, there was a large room on the left which was the main living/reception room. It had large windows to the front and back overlooking the garden, which was a long grassed area with tall hedges either side, very private. The living room was simply furnished, sparse, neat and tidy, a tall cupboard by the open fireplace, dining chairs lined up against the wall to the garden which were brought out and arranged around the small table at mealtimes. Off this room was the kitchen with a window and door to the garden.
>
> 'The other room downstairs was smaller, used as a store room, with all sorts of things piled up haphazardly! This is the room where Grand-père showed me his First World War uniform jacket with the hole in the shoulder.
>
> 'The house felt quite different to my other grandparents' house and my experiences there were also different. For example drinking red wine like cordial with water at lunch! The food looked and tasted different. On arrival the first thing Grand-mère would do was put her arm around my shoulder and guide me to her special cupboard by the fireplace in the living room. This was extremely exciting as I knew there would be something in there for me. It was always a food surprise, maybe chocolate, maybe a beautiful cake, but always a brand or type I'd never seen before. This is also where she kept the coffee grinder, another exciting thing for me as I knew she would give me the very important and responsible job of grinding the coffee beans. The grinder was the small square wooden box type with grinding handle on the top, drawer underneath. It was light and compact, perfect for my small hands. It seemed like a miracle that the drawer would at first be empty, but

within a few simple grinds of the handle, the drawer would fill with coffee ready for brewing and which always smelt wonderful. Maybe it's part of the reason I still love freshly ground coffee!

'I had a sense that even though Grand-mère and I couldn't communicate, she would include me. Grinding the coffee and stirring butter into the pan with the petit pois, both seemed like really important jobs with a lot of responsibility for someone as young as me. The butter in the peas seemed really luxurious and excessive but I loved the outcome – they were totally delicious.'

Family was hugely important to Yvonne, even though her outspokenness had a tendency to suggest the opposite and push her children away. As adults, her children still found her exasperating, never knowing whether on any given day she would be charming or difficult, a worry when it came to weddings and other family gatherings. Mostly they kept their distance, particularly if Yvonne had been less than friendly towards their spouses.

If she found being 'Mum' difficult, it appears she more easily enjoyed being '*Grand-mère*' and cared greatly about her grandchildren. In 1957, Gordon and his family emigrated to Canada. Soon after they arrived, in the depths of winter, one of their children fell quite seriously ill. It was a worrying and difficult time, compounded with the challenges of getting established in a new country and finding somewhere permanent to live. Yvonne became very concerned and wrote plaintively in June 1959:

'Dear Gordon, dear Joan, dear children,
 We are all worried we have had no news from you, be good enough both of you to tell us how you and the children are. Is Bernard better, poor little one... Cynthia and Stanley came on holiday... and Cynthia, who has a heart of gold, immediately gave us your address. Tell us how you are doing and if you need anything. Hoping you will be good enough to tell us a little about your children. Lift the hearts of your parents.
Mum, Dad & Eric xxx'

('Mon cher Gordon, ma cherie Joan, chers enfants,
 Nous somme tous dans l'ennui de n'avoir pas de vos nouvelles, soyez bon tous les deux comment vous êtes avec les enfants. Bernard est-il mieux, pauvre petit Cynthia et Stanley sont venu en vacances et aussitôt Cynthia, qui a un coeur d'or, nous a donné votre addresse. Dites nous comment est votre situation, si il faut faire quelque chose pour vous. Ésperant que vous serez assez bon de nous dire un peu de vos enfants. Haute les coeurs de vos parents.

23: LEAVING FRANCE

Mum, Dad & Eric xxx')

Yvonne uses an interesting turn of expression in her letter when she says '*soyez bon tous les deux*'. This is not a phrase a French person would use. It is as if she has translated from English a phrase she has heard: 'be good enough both of you'. This suggests her understanding of English was much better than she let on.

The years flowed by, with Albert steadfastly by Yvonne's side. She never let go of the hope they might return to live in France, but had to content herself with the annual visits to Allery, where her friends the Allots still lived. The Allots had experienced their own ups and downs over the years. In the 1960s, the family jute manufacturing business fell into terminal decline, the result of overseas competition, and Louis retired in 1968. His daughter Nadette and her husband Marcel Defente opened a restaurant in Allery in 1965. They built it on land the family owned on the outskirts of the village and named it Le Pont d'Hure.[26] Paule Allot died in 1980 and Louis in 1992. They are buried together in the graveyard in Allery.

Forever longing for France, Yvonne did not integrate well into British life. It is astonishing that in more than 45 years in Hertfordshire she never spoke English. At first, perhaps, she did not believe they would stay long enough to worry about learning the language, yet as time rolled on, she continued to resist speaking anything except French. The reason may have been a profound lack of confidence or, perhaps more likely, an act of resistance.

Ron and his wife June remember Yvonne often saying she hated the English language, the English people and England itself. She frequently talked of 'when we go back to France'. Her unwillingness to speak the language made it more difficult for her to get to know people and for the family to assimilate into the local community.

In any case, Yvonne did not welcome visitors to the house. This included anyone her children brought home and Albert's extended family. She tried to stand firmly between Albert and his siblings, including his sister Catherine who lived close by. Albert's mother, Mary, who was widowed in 1930, seldom saw her grandchildren. (She died in 1960.) It was as if Yvonne was afraid they would find out about her past and come between her and Albert. Utterly dependant on him, and harbouring deep insecurities, she guarded him fiercely.

---

[26] Run by their son Frédéric in recent decades, it closed at the end of 2020 when Frédéric retired.

Perhaps the powerful patriotism of First World War France gave rise to Yvonne's strong attachment to the country of her birth, despite her tough early life there. Motherless, she at least had a Motherland. Or maybe it was just that she yearned for the familiar, after so many changes and moves forced on her at a young age. She even found the culinary culture shock of England hard to bear, arriving at a time of wartime tinned Spam, boiled cabbage and disappointing tomatoes. She rightly claimed French tomatoes were bigger and had more flavour.

Yvonne did eventually fulfil her dream to live in France again, but only after Albert's death in April 1985. By now the houses in Athelstan Walk, which had been built with experimental but cheap methods using concrete panels, had been condemned. The walls had bowed and there were issues with severe damp. In total, 500 houses in the area were demolished in the mid-1980s as part of a redevelopment programme. All that remains of Athelstan Walk today is the name, given to a street of new houses and flats running parallel to Broadwater Road.

Losing her husband of over sixty years and her home of more than forty-five years was a double blow, no doubt prompting Yvonne's return to France. Leaving behind her large family, which by now included great-grandchildren, she moved across the English Channel to Boulogne-sur-Mer. She rented an apartment at Residence Les Oiseaux, 63 boulevard Mariette. The building is still there today, a white-painted block in a row of similar buildings, housing six apartments. It faces the walls of Boulogne's old town, with its 13th-century ramparts. Directly behind the buildings there is an attractive public park but it is doubtful Yvonne spent much time there. It is on a very steep site with lots of steps, not easily accessible for older people.

The town held good memories for Yvonne of the early days of her marriage, when she, Albert and baby Gordon lived in neighbouring Wimereux, and of family holidays in the 1930s. However, the decision to move there was unusual and brave. She was a recently-widowed woman in her mid-eighties, not in the best of health, and hadn't lived in France for well over 45 years. It is believed her youngest son Eric, then in his 40s, helped her move and settle in. After that, how she managed alone in Boulogne no one remembers. Her home was in a hilly part of town and not very convenient for the shops and amenities she needed.

Yvonne told her family she wished to end her days in France and she did. Outliving Albert by just two years, she passed away at the age of 86 in hospital in Boulogne-sur-Mer on 6 July 1987. Yet Yvonne was not buried on her beloved French soil. She was laid to rest on 20 July 1987 along-

23: LEAVING FRANCE

side Albert and their daughter Heather, in the cemetery on the outskirts of Welwyn Garden City. She lies for all eternity with family, never to be separated again, at the end of an extraordinary life.

63 boulevard Mariette today (3rd building from right): Yvonne's final home, in Boulogne-sur-Mer

Epilogue: Searching for Marie

MARIE MATERIALISES FROM the mists of history in 1900, vanishes again in early 1905 and leaves no trails behind her. The only clue to where she came from lies in the register of women admitted to the maternity ward at the Hôtel-Dieu in 1901. Archivists gave me access to the original document at the AP-HP Archives in Paris in October 2018. It states Marie was 28 years old and was born in the commune of Annecy, Haute-Savoie, in the French Alps.

Annecy is the principal town, or commune, in the arrondissement (administrative area) of Annecy, which comprises 93 communes in total. If Marie was aged 28 when Yvonne was born on 11 June 1901, her own date of birth was between 11 June 1872 and 11 June 1873. I looked at all the birth records available online for the town of Annecy and to be sure, all the communes in the wider arrondissement of Annecy, for 1872 and 1873. I even searched 1871 and 1874, just in case there had been a mistake made on the hospital record. Although there were some potential matches, they led down blind alleys to dead ends. I could not find Marie.

In January 2019, the discovery Marie had given birth to another daughter, a year before Yvonne was born, prompted a rethink. The record of Henriette Yvonne Marie Louise's birth on 29 March 1900, which I found on the Paris Archive's website, states her mother's age was 29. If correct, Marie was at least 30 years old when she gave birth to Yvonne in June 1901. It would mean Marie was born sometime between 29 March 1870 and 29 March 1871. The records for the births of Marie's two daughters cannot both be accurate.

I went online again to the Haute-Savoie archives, this time widening the search to the *'tables decennales'* for the whole of the Annecy arrondissement between the years 1863 to 1883. The *'tables decennales'* list all births alphabetically by decade for each commune. There was no strong match for our Marie Millet anywhere. Searching all the communes in the wider Annecy area was, in any case, a long shot. The 1901 hospital record says that she was born in the 'commune' of Annecy, in other words, in the town of Annecy itself.

EPILOGUE: SEARCHING FOR MARIE

Millet was an unusual name in the Haute-Savoie in the late 19th century. This helped with the search because there are few people by that name to be checked out. Ironically, it is quite a common name in north-eastern France, where Yvonne spent the first 38 years of her life.

In the town of Annecy itself, there were only six Millet births between 1863-83 and none of them were girls with the name Marie. Among the communes of Annecy, I found Caroline-Marie Millet born in Entrevernes in April 1872, who was 29 on 11 June 1901, but the name is not quite right. Marie Lucia Millet from Hauteville-sur-Fler and Marie-Franceline Millet from Lathuile, both born in October 1873, were only 27 on 11 June 1901, making both too young to be likely candidates. Marie-Jeanette Millet from Le Bouchet was born in December 1874, was only 26 on 11 June 1901, so is also an unconvincing match.

The most promising lead was Marie-Seudonie Millet from Saint-Jorioz, born in April 1873. Not only did her birth date fit with the Hôtel-Dieu register, but records showed that at the age of 26 she was working as a *cuisinière* in Lyon, France's third largest city. It was not too much a stretch of the imagination to place her working as a *cuisinière* in Paris in 1901. The fact she returned home to Saint-Jorioz to marry a local man in 1899 did not rule her out completely. There was no trace of either of them in Saint-Jorioz on the census of 1901 or 1906 – they were obviously both living elsewhere, Paris maybe? I started to wonder if the marriage had failed, and Marie had even moved to Paris alone to a new position by 1900, where the following year she had a baby.

Unfortunately, I had not found the right woman. The couple reappeared on the 1911 census for Saint-Jorioz, by which time they had two daughters, one of which was born in July 1901 in another commune of Annecy. Marie Millet of Saint-Jorioz was not the Marie Millet who gave birth to Yvonne in Paris in June 1901, despite the uncanny parallels. The person I had found was another Annecy woman who happened to be of the right age, name, and profession and who also gave birth to a daughter the same summer. The records went on to reveal that Marie Millet of Saint-Jorioz was a more fortunate woman from a large family, who married well, raised her children and lived the rest of her life in Saint-Jorioz, surrounded by the beauty of the mountains.

Archivists told me mistakes were frequently made on hospital registers in the early 20th century. This knowledge led down a new path of exploration. I wondered if the entry for Marie's maternity stay was muddled with the mother on the next line of the 1900 register. She was also called Marie

– Marie Ducret – and was also a *cuisinière* of much the same age. It is easy to imagine a sloppy clerk mixing the details of the two women.

Marie Ducret's birthplace is shown as Aymavilles in the Italian Alps. On a hunch, I made enquiries with the archive service in Aymavilles to see if they could find Marie Millet in the town's birth records. They could not. But they did say Millet is a fairly common surname in the Aosta Valley and normally Marie was followed by other first names. There are also many Millets in Switzerland who emigrated from the Aosta Valley. Together with the results of a DNA test taken by Yvonne's grandson Chris Bagley, which suggest southern European ancestry, it seems likely Marie was indeed from somewhere in the Alps. Perhaps she was descended from an Italian or Swiss family rather than French.

We may never know with certainty her true origins.

A generation before Yvonne's birth…

Extract from *Europe Viewed Through American Spectacles* by Charles C. Fulton, written in 1873

THE OFFICIAL RETURNS of the hospitals of Paris show that of the fifty-five thousand births in the city during the past year, fifteen thousand three hundred and sixty-six were illegitimate. The proportion of illegitimates to the number of inhabitants is not quite up to that of Vienna, which has ten thousand for one million inhabitants, whilst the population of Paris is nearly two million. In various parts of Paris, boxes called 'tours' are established, each of which revolves upon a pivot, and, on a bell being rung, is turned around by the person inside to receive the child that may have been deposited in it without attempting to ascertain who the parents are.

The child is taken to a hospital and cared for, and as soon as a nurse from the country may be procured, it is given into her charge. Nurses from the country, of good character, are always applying for these infants. The nurses are paid by the city from four francs to eight francs per month, according to the age of the child, care being taken to assign the children to nurses living as far as possible from their birthplaces. After the second year, the nurse may give the child up, when, if no other nurse can be found for it, it is transferred to the Orphan Department. Sometimes the nurses become so attached to the children that they retain them. The number of children thus placed out in the country to nurse is about four thousand annually. The abolition, in some of the departments, of this humane custom of receiving these little waifs and asking no questions has caused infanticide to become very frequent. As for infanticide before birth, the number is said to have doubled and trebled in some districts, and to have risen to four and five times the usual amount in others. The average number of foundlings maintained at the Paris Hospital is four thousand four hundred. At the age of twelve, the boys are bound apprentice to some trade at the expense of the city. A portion of one hundred and forty-eight francs is awarded by the city to female foundlings when they marry, provided their conduct has been unexceptionable throughout.

The Hospice des Enfants Assistés founded in 1640 by St. Vincent of Paul is for the reception of foundlings. For a child to be received at this hospital, however, it is necessary that a certificate of abandonment be produced, signed by a Commissary of Police. The Commissary is bound to admonish the mother or party abandoning the child and to procure for them assistance from the hospital fund in case of their consenting to retain and support the child. Every encouragement is thus given to those who relinquish the idea of abandoning their offspring and consent to support them at home. Of the children received at this hospital, those that are healthy are put out in the country to nurse, whilst those that are sickly are retained at the hospital until they die or recover. The number of beds in this hospital is about six hundred. And the children annually sent from it to the country are about four thousand three hundred. The children are first placed in a general reception room, called La Crêche, where they are visited every morning by the physicians assigned to the different infirmaries. In each of these infirmaries, as well as in La Crêche, cradles are placed around the walls in rows, and several nurses are constantly employed in attending to them. An inclined bed is placed in front of the fire, on which the children who require it are laid, and chairs are ranged in a warm corner, in which those of sufficient age and strength sit part of the day.

Everything is admirably conducted, and to all outward appearances they are kindly and humanely cared for.

Selected Bibliography

Abandoned Children, Foundlings and child welfare in Nineteenth-Century France
Rachel G Fuchs

Abbeville et son arrondissement pendant la Guerre (août 1914-novembre 1918)
Chanoine Le Sueur
Held in the collections of the Archives et Bibliothèque Patrimoniale d'Abbeville

Ces ancêtres oublié: Domestiques, nousnous, gens de maison
Marie-Odile Mergnac

Femmes d'Allery
Bernadette Defente

Harry Patch, The Last Fighting Tommy
Harry Patch with Richard Van Emden

Jean et Yvonne, Domestiques en 1900
Paul Chabot

La Vie des Domestiques en France au XIXe Siècle
Pierre Guiral & Guy Thuillier

Les droits de l'enfant abandonné (1811-2003)
Ivan Jablonka, Maitre de conferences, Université du Maines - Le Mans

Mad Enchantment, Claude Monet and the painting of the Water Lilies
Ross King

Paris, Biography of a City
Colin Jones

Poor & Pregnant in Paris, Strategies for Survival in the Nineteenth Century
Rachel G Fuchs

The Pain and the Privilege: The Women Who Loved Lloyd George
Ffion Hague

The Soldier's War: The Great War Through Veterans' Eyes
Richard Van Emden

William An Englishman
Cicely Hamilton, 1919, Persephone Books

Websites:

forces-war-records.co.uk/units/4899/london-regiment/

archives.hautesavoie.fr/

archive.org/stream/lhoteldieupario0fossuoft#page/254/mode/2up

allery.fr/index.php/commune/histoire
(photos of Allery)

alphadeltaplus.20m.com/
(information about Canon Row police station)

20thlondon.com/

thehistorypress.co.uk/articles/evacuation-of-the-wounded-in-world-war-i/

ourwelwyngardencity.org.uk/

paris-a-nu.fr/le-moulin-de-la-galette-vu-par-les-peintres/
(history of the Moulin de la Gal Paris)

Index

Abandonment of children: 42–43, 45, 61–62, 66, 81, 153, 169, 206
Abbeville: 4, 74, 76, 78, 99–100, 105–114, 117–119, 121–126, 129–132, 136–138, 140–144, 149, 151, 153, 158, 162, 165–169, 171–172, 175, 178, 184, 192, 207
   Hôtel de Ville: 171–173
   port: 106, 117, 166, 168, 175
   station: 74, 106
Adoption of children: 36
Airaines: 149–152
Albert (town): 45, 49, 52, 56–57, 119
Allery: 6–7, 9, 71, 74, 76–81, 84–87, 90–91, 97, 99–101, 104–105, 112, 133, 143–144, 149, 151, 163, 174–175, 189, 193, 195–196, 199, 207–208
   jute manufacturing: 78–79, 87, 199
   Quayet neighbourhood: 76, 80, 86–87, 89, 163, 195
   school: 86
Allot, Louis: 6, 79, 87–88, 189, 193, 195
Amiens: 4–5, 12, 59, 66–69, 74–75, 77, 85, 105–108, 119, 121, 126, 131–132, 144–146, 148–150, 152–153, 162, 184
Annecy (Haute Savoie): 21–22, 65, 202–203
Années Folles: 158
AP-HP: 4, 21, 202
Artists, Montmartre
   Picasso, Pablo: 18, 33, 87
   Renoir, Pierre-Auguste: 33
   Toulouse-Lautrec, Henri: 33
   Utrillo, Maurice: 33
   Van Dongen, Kees: 33

Assistance Publique: 41–42, 44–45, 49, 59, 61, 66–67, 74, 83–85, 90, 104–105, 109, 111, 124, 131, 139–140, 143–145, 149, 151, 154–155, 162–163, 176–177
   inspection visits: 81, 124
   social workers: 12, 89, 111, 144, 153, 155
   welfare payments: 44–45, 62
Bagley, family: 2, 6, 9, 11, 92–93, 96, 101, 119–121, 127–128, 135, 165, 174, 182–186, 188, 190–191, 193–194, 197, 204
baptism: 89
Battles, Great War
   Albert: 128
   Amiens: 132
   Loos: 96
   Transloy Ridges: 120
Belgium: 97, 122, 128, 133, 164, 178, 183, 186, 189
Belle Époque, La: 7, 16, 19
Billet: see Desjardins
Blackheath (Woolwich): 92–93, 147
bonne à tout faire: 26
Boucher, Abbé: 89–90
Boulogne-sur-Mer: 82, 85, 178, 184–185, 200–201
   Pierre Napoléon: 178–179
Bourdon, Marguerite: 88, 175
bourgeoisie: 19, 24–26, 30–31, 81
British army: 55, 106, 113, 191–192
Bussus-Bussuel: 140–144, 148–149

Caisse d'Épargne: 105
Cassel (Flanders): 95
Cenotaph, Whitehall: 159–160
Chabot, Paul: 9, 36, 207
childcare: 37–38, 49

Childcare
  bottle feeding: 56
  breast feeding: 43, 48, 56
  nourrices: 49–51, 59
  nurseries: 38
Church
  Notre-Dame cathedral (Paris): 40
  Sainte-Trinité (Allery): 78, 84, 89–90, 112, 184, 194
  Saint-François (Roubaix): 184, 186
  Saint-Julien-le-Pauvre (Paris): 43
  Saint-Martin (Croix): 186
  St Bonaventure, Welwyn Garden City: 190–191
Cinema
  Film pioneers: 63
  Gaumont, Léon: 63
  Lumière brothers: 63
  Méliès, George: 63
  Pathé, Charles and Emile: 63
Clemenceau, George: 136
Crécy-en-Ponthieu: 123
cuisinière: 22, 26–28, 32, 39, 45, 53, 140, 154, 203–204

Dallon, Louis: 108–109, 118, 123
Dambourgez, Edouard-Jean: 29
Demobilisation: 126, 134
Desjardins, Alfred and Valentine: 6, 74–77, 80, 82–85, 98–101, 105, 112, 137, 143–144, 149, 151, 158, 162–163, 169, 174–176, 182, 195
Domestic service: See Domestiques
domestiques: 9, 19, 21, 23–28, 31, 33–37, 39, 48, 63–64, 67, 85, 108, 118, 125, 137, 140, 148–149, 177, 207
Domestiques
  daily life: 60, 75, 78, 84, 137, 153, 168
  unemployment: 64, 159, 177
  working hours: 28, 38, 109, 148
Dubois, Doctor Léon: 152

education: 85, 89–90, 163
Entertainment
  dances: 33, 148, 158

femme de chambre: 26–27, 30–31, 37–40
Festubert (Pas-de-Calais): 95, 101
Foch, Maréchal: 132, 136, 167, 172
foster care: 73, 81, 85, 118, 144, 163

Genet, Jean: 81
Great War, The: 16, 24, 54, 136, 150, 159, 207
  Armistice: 55, 133, 136, 160
  Battle of the Somme: 55, 117–118, 122
  Gas attacks: 126
  Hindenberg Line: 126–127
  Spring Offensive: 130
  Treaty of Versailles: 136–137
  Veterinary hospitals, Abbeville: 110
  Voluntary work: 125
  War Diary: 93–94, 122, 133

Haig, General: 132
Hitler, Adolf: 137
hospices: 4, 67, 144, 184
Hospices
  Filles de la Charité de Saint Vincent de Paul: 4, 67, 107
  Saint-Charles, Amiens: 5, 66–69, 73, 144–145, 149
  Sister Jeanne: 108, 124, 153
Hôtel-Dieu, Paris: 40–43, 202–203

infant mortality: 36, 49–50

Kitchener, Lord: 91

Lainière, La: 183–184
Le Havre: 95–96, 134
Lemaire: 138–139
Leroy, Paul and family: 125–126, 130–131, 133, 136
Le Sueur, Canon (Chanoine): 109–110, 207
Lille: 5, 13, 96, 133, 152, 175, 183, 185, 188, 190
  textile industry: 175, 188
Lloyd George, David: 136, 207
Lloyds of London: 135
London: 2, 4–5, 19, 28–29, 65, 91–93, 97, 120, 122, 134–137, 141, 147, 158, 164–166, 168, 178, 186, 188, 192, 197
London Regiment, 20th Battalion: 93, 120, 166
Loos: 96

MacGuire, Denis: 167–168
Magnier, Esther: 145–146, 148–149, 152
marriage: 7, 10, 12–13, 28, 35, 50, 65, 157, 162–163, 167–168, 171–176, 178, 182, 200, 203

INDEX

maternity: 21–22, 39, 41–44, 202–203
Maternity
    care available: 42, 128
    financial support, welfare: 35, 38, 41, 44–45, 61–62, 64, 82, 111, 124, 207
    pregnancy: 35–39, 170–171
    single parenting: 34, 174
Médaille de la Famille française: 182
Metropolitan Police: 5–6, 147–148, 158–159, 165
    Canon Row Police Station: 147, 159, 208
military cemetery: 134
Millet
    Henriette Yvonne Marie Louise (sister of Yvonne): 34–35, 37, 42–44, 49, 51–53, 65, 89, 202
    Marie (mother of Yvonne): 7, 16–35, 37–45, 48–49, 51–54, 56–65, 73, 75, 80–81, 87, 89, 104, 123, 125, 131, 153–154, 167, 174, 176–177, 187, 202–204
Morisot, Berthe: 48
Mouret, Anatole and Martine: 154
Mullier, Albert and Charlotte: 80, 195

Nazis: 189–190
Nourrices
    bottle feeding: 56
    rules governing: 50
    wet nurses: 56

Orwell, George: 19, 28

Pandemic, influenza: 89, 132
Paris
    Eiffel Tower: 17
    Exposition Universelle: 17–18
    Les Halles, market: 23, 29, 39
    metro: 17
    Montmartre: 18, 33
    Notre Dame cathedral: 40
    rue Berger: 22–24, 27, 29, 31–32, 34, 37–38, 40, 42, 53, 62
    rue de Rivoli: 16–17, 31
    Square René-Viviani: 41
Patch, Harry: 119, 134, 207
Paternity
    laws relating to responsibility: 35, 44
Pickett, F.N. et Fils, Wimereux: 4, 178, 183

Poccardi, Marguerite: 87–89, 133
Poiret, family: 80
Pregnancy: See Maternity
Prix Cognacq-Jay: 182

Raymond, family: 153
Renoir, Pierre-Auguste: 33
    Bal au Moulin de la Galette, painting: 33
Ricaut, family: 149–152
Roper, Thomas: 166, 172
Roubaix: 183–186

Saint-Valery-sur-Somme: 85, 168
scabies: 129–130
Second World War: 151, 172, 191, 193, 197
    Luftwaffe: 172
Servants: See Domestiques
Shakespeare and Company, bookshop, Paris: 41
Sixièmes, les: 7, 21, 23, 28, 42
Somme
    Battle of the Somme: 55, 117–118, 122
    Bay of the Somme: 84, 168
    River Somme: 76, 106, 117, 125, 175

Talon, Victorine: 49–62, 64–66, 69, 82, 176
Thiepval (Somme): 5, 7, 47, 49–51, 53–57, 60–62, 65–66, 75, 79, 82, 89, 117, 125, 130, 159, 176
Thuillier, Paul Marie Joseph: 50, 57, 123–124, 145–146, 149, 207
Tourcoing: 185–186
Treaty of Versailles: 136–137
tuberculosis: 64

Verne, Jules: 5, 68
Vimy Ridge (Pas-de-Calais): 119

Welwyn Garden City: 188, 191–192, 195, 197, 201
    Athelstan Walk: 188–189, 191–193, 197, 200
    ICI Plastics: 191
    Murphy Radio: 191
Wilson, Woodrow: 136
Wimereux (Pas-de-Calais): 178–179, 184, 186, 200

ABOUT THE AUTHOR

Sara Rowell began writing thanks to a chance conversation with a friend, after a career in marketing and communications. She is fascinated by stories within ordinary families at extraordinary points in history, and how they can echo down the generations. A member of Solihull Writers (solihullwriters.co.uk), her writing includes historical biography and historical fiction. In 2020 and 2022 she won the Solihull Writers non-fiction competition.